NE

STRAIGHT TALK FROM PRISON

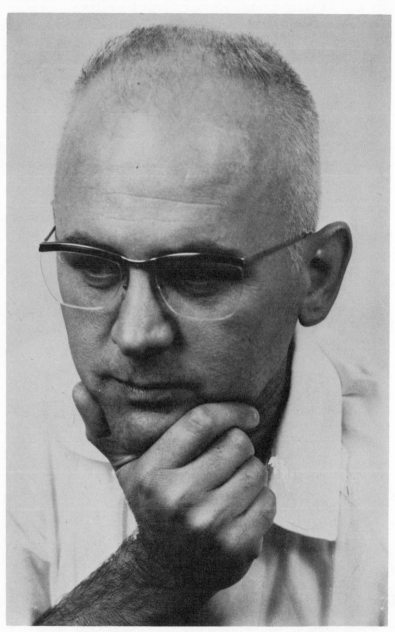

Lou Torok, the "Convict Writer"

STRAIGHT TALK FROM PRISON

A Convict Reflects on Youth, Crime and Society

by

Lou Torok

NEWTON COUNTY LIBRARY

Human Sciences Press • New York

A Division of Behavioral Publications, Inc.

Library of Congress Catalog Number 74-1074

ISBN: 0-87705-136-4

Copyright © 1974 by Human Sciences Press

All rights reserved. No part of this work may be reproduced or utilized in any form or by any means, electronic or mechanical, including photocopying, microfilm and recording, or by any information storage and retrieval system without permission in writing from the publisher.

Human Sciences Press is a division of Behavioral Publications, 72 Fifth Avenue, New York, New York 10011

Printed in the United States of America
456789   987654321

Variations of the material appearing in quotes have appeared in *The Cincinatti Enquirer, The Fort Worth Star Telegram, King Features' Syndicate* and other newspapers syndicated throughout the United States.

NEWTON COUNTY LIBRARY   NC 74-138
.364.3

Library of Congress Cataloging in Publication Data

Torok, Lou.
    Straight talk from prison.

    1. Prisons. 2. Crime and criminals. 3. Criminal justice, Administration of. I. Title.
HV8665.T67   364   74-1074

CONTENTS

PHOTO CREDITS

Photographs on pp. 2, 14, 18, 22, 26, 38, 51, 99, and 108, courtesy of Ted R. Schneider, Jr., *Akron Beacon Journal*

Photograph on p. 63, courtesy of the National Council on Crime and Delinquency

Photograph on p. 115, courtesy of the Department of Corrections, City of New York

FOREWORD

MILTON G. RECTOR
*President, National Council on
Crime and Delinquency*

For a variety of reasons young people today tend to distrust age and authority and to listen more intently to what they consider the authentic, genuine article. Official preachments they regard as commandments stamped in plastic and they shun them with a vengeance. Perhaps they are right.

The great value of Lou Torok's sensible and compassionate advice in this book is that it comes from the genuine man, and because it does it has an acceptability that the policeman, minister, and teacher may only aspire to but seldom reach. Torok has sinned and suffered. Part of his atonement is to urge youth and their parents with resounding conviction that crime is a dead end.

If fathers could speak to sons like Torok does to his readers—without preachiness and sanctimony—the message would have a far better chance of getting through. For Torok's simple, unadorned description

of the sounds and smells of prison must give one
pause. For juvenile or adult, each page flashes a
warning about criminal acts that only the blind could
blink aside.

His explanation of how the adolescent can so easily
take the path that leads to crime and the grim re-
wards of doing so is thoroughly convincing. His own
personal experience of youthful crime and later of
coming to understand himself realistically and ma-
turely in prison, and of finding a way to keep his spirit
intact despite steel bars and high walls, is an inspiring
story.

There is more than one message in *Straight Talk
from Prison*. There is, of course, the very graphic
warning of what crime does to the body and spirit.
But there is also a genuine effort to describe what
crime really is, and how easily—almost unwittingly—
some may enter it. And finally there is a good description of that big, bungling, inefficient, and often
unjust thing which we call the criminal justice system. Torok points out how despite the best of inten-
tions it so often fails not only the criminal but the
public as well.

He explains, more succinctly and convincingly
than would a text twice the length of his book, how
early up-bringing, the lack of parental care, and the
absence of love are the building blocks of a criminal
personality. If there is a sermon in these pages at all,
it is that parents must love their children, but that
this love must be reinforced by good example and
responsible direction.

Considering Torok's experiences in prison, his
view of the system is charitable. He believes that it

is possible for the prison to reform and redirect the offender. Perhaps this happens in the rare instance. It is certainly not common. That Torok himself has emerged with his psyche intact and with a determination to help others avoid imprisonment is indeed a persuasive argument lending credence to the fact that a person can rehabilitate himself in prison.

If Lou Torok deliberately set out to write an *apologia pro sua vita* he could not have done better than to place it in the framework of this useful book. For its simple, direct language and its unvarnished realism and frankness must be a deterrent to any youth who has the good fortune to leaf through its pages. There is no doubt in my mind that Torok long ago paid his debt to society. But with this book and its promise for helping young people and informing their parents, he has earned more than redemption; he has earned the right to be called teacher and guide. And that is precisely how he emerges in *Straight Talk from Prison.*

ACKNOWLEDGEMENTS

A Debt of Honor . . .

When I first walked out of San Quentin Prison on parole in 1950, there was no one to greet me. Nobody cared whether I was free or not.

Fifteen years later, when I was paroled from the Maine State Prison, nobody greeted me at the gate. I was still a loner and had no one who really cared that much about me.

But things were different in 1972, when I walked out of the Chillicothe (Ohio) Correctional Institute. There to greet me and make me feel welcome once again in the outside world were Mrs. Ruth Voss, Young People Editor of the *Cincinnati Enquirer* and her five year old son, Joey. They engulfed me in a blanket of love and concern that helped me to change my life. Little Joey was so excited about sharing my new freedom that he got an upset stomach.

In the first difficult months of my freedom I was made to feel welcome at the Voss home in Sharonville, Ohio. Little did it matter that there were eight Voss children and a lovable German Shepherd, "Bruta," to share in all this love.

I am truly free at last because of the love and faith and trust of Ruth and Bob Voss and their eight beautiful children.

Under the circumstances "thank you" seems like such a small thing to say for so much.

Letter to My Son

~~~~~~

"Dear Son,

When I broke the law and ended up in prison, I didn't know how much it would hurt you and your mother. Now I am not there to help you. I wish I could stand beside you when the kids at school call you "jailbird's kid" but I can't be there because I am in prison. That is why I am writing this book: to help you help yourself.

This is not the first time I have broken the law. I actually started my life of crime when I was your age. I began by stealing candy bars from the grocery store. It was fun, it was easy and I got away with it.

Scenes of the grounds of Chillicothe Correctional Institute, Lou Torok's home for three years.

One day, however, I was caught. I told the grocer I had "forgotten" to pay for the stuff. He let me go. That grocer showed me how easy it was to con a sympathetic "bleeding-heart" adult. How I wish now he had punished me, called the police or my parents. I thought the grocer was a pushover. I thought the cops were a bunch of fools. I thought I was the only one who had any brains because I was getting away with things.

I found out how easy it was to get into houses when the owners were away. Already I was headed for the big time and didn't even know it. I used to cut classes at school and go on the prowl with my own gang. I felt like a real man when I stole someone's valuables.

As a teenager I tried everything for thrills. If it had been easy to get hard drugs in those days I would have tried them. As it was, I got plenty of beer whenever I wanted it and even hard liquor. I am sure that kids today are finding it just as easy to get drugs as we did to get booze.

There will be many times when you will hate me for what I've done to you and your mother. Please don't waste your hate on me. Instead, learn to hate the cruelty and indifference that hide behind the masks of ordinary peoples' faces. Learn to hate the poverty that makes so many people turn to crime as a way of fulfilling their basic needs. Hate the ignorance that allows a child to drop out of school before he is properly prepared to earn a living. Learn to hate the prejudice in all people that makes them suspicious of anyone who does not think, dress, talk like them or go to the same church they do. Learn to hate those who preach hatred.

Son, I don't want you to end up like me, in prison. If you are looking for a thrill to pass the time, if you break the law, any law, even if you get away with it at first, it may eventually cost you a lifetime behind bars. Don't risk it. Please think about what I am saying to you."

Love,
Dad

For the Record

When I met Jimmie Angel twenty-five years ago in San Quentin Prison, I was shocked by the tatoo etched on his arm.

"Born to lose."

He was eighteen and I was twenty. We were both getting our start in life as losers.

Today, over twenty-five years later ... and after spending time in three prisons in California, Maine, and Ohio ... I still feel there is hope.

But some men have abandoned all hope. For them, the prison experience is the end of a road that started out leading nowhere. During my years in and out of

17

Lou Torok in his cell at the Chillicothe Correctional Institute in Ohio, which doubled as an office for the budding convict writer.

prisons around the country I have met thousands of convicts. If one thing could characterize them it would have to be that they were failures. They were failures at life and living. They were failures in human relations. They were failures in school, in business, at work, at home, everywhere. The final indignity was that they were even now failures at crime—they got caught.

One of the primary motivations that prodded me into writing from behind prison bars ... and even now as a paroled convict living in the free world ... is the hope that somehow I can put the finger of America on the pulse of the "typical" convict, if such a being does exist. I want people everywhere to take an unglossed and non-glamorous look at the criminals and social failures who inhabit our prisons.

To do this it has been necessary for me to put my own story "on front street" as we say in convict slang. This meant that I had to give up the protective anonymity that I had spent twenty-five years building like a cocoon around myself and my criminal past.

In the beginning, prison officials were shocked that I would come forth in so brazen a manner and cautioned me that I was taking a sizeable risk in calling myself "The Convict Writer." What they did not know was that over the past twenty-five years a consistent pattern emerged in which I would be totally destroyed economically and socially on those occasions when my criminal past was discovered. What they did not know was that I was tired of hiding. What they did not know was that in order to communicate honestly and effectively with ordinary concerned people it was necessary for me to take a certain risk and to declare myself. So, what I did was point out that my public criminal record was now a thing of the past ... and that after leaving prison I would try to keep it that way.

If anybody could be said to have been "born to lose" I am that person. On August 7, 1927 I was born in the Florence Crittenden home in Toledo, Ohio. Because my Hungarian parents and grand-parents could not forget the bitter political fight between Catholic and Protestant Hungarians that they supposedly left Hungary to escape, I was physically threatened as a new-born infant. At eleven days of age, the Lucas County Court made me a ward of the court. Thus it was that I began my life under the orders of the court and would spend most of my life under such orders.

I spent all of my childhood in orphanages and boarding schools without love, without affection, without close personal relationships. This hunger for acceptance and for deep, personal, and intimate love has followed me every day of my life. I suspect it has been the principal reason for the "acting out" of my repressed aggressions throughout my life, leading me into so many difficult and trying extra-legal activities. Not until I discovered writing as a way of relieving these frustrations would I know real happiness.

As "The Convict Writer" my articles, books, plays and even a "New World Prayer" would impress thousands of persons all over the world. My writing brought mail from every country in the world, including Russia, Red China, and from many obscure places difficult to find on a map.

Mostly, however, the mail came from people in the United States who were deeply touched by my attempt to "talk straight" and who wanted to let me know how much it meant to them.

What all this did to me—and for me—was to give me an entirely new outlook on life. It gave me a reason for living. It gave me a purpose. It restored my faith. It gave me hope once again. I did not have to be "born to lose."

When the parole board heard my case in July, 1972 they rejected me for parole. But then suddenly in September, less than three months later, they reconsidered and granted me a parole. Certainly my writing efforts and the thousands of letters written by ordinary citizens to Governor John J. Gilligan, and to the Ohio Adult Parole Authority in my behalf, did not hurt my case.

But perhaps most important, I had learned a significant lesson contained in an encouraging letter to me from one of my first "fans," Kay Besold of Oak Park, Illinois. This lesson was "grow where you are." It was this thought and the dynamic power it unleashed that enabled me to risk everything to begin a new career as a writer under nearly impossible conditions. There were others who stimulated me to write. A broken-hearted mother from Marblehead, Ohio had written to share her grief and to lament the fact that had she but seen "A Convict's Letter to His Son" a week earlier things may have turned out less tragically. She wrote to tell me that she had just returned from the cemetery, having just buried her sixteen year old son. He and a group of friends had robbed a gas station "for kicks" and were climbing

Mr. Torok, shortly before his release, strolling on the grounds of
Chillicothe . . . and in a more pensive mood

out of the window when the police arrived. The police called for the youths to stop and proceeded to fire a warning shot over their heads. One shot went wild and struck this woman's son in the back. He was killed instantly. Deeply moved by this tragic tale, penned on tear-stained paper, I was further inspired to proceed with my writing.

If I thought I could reach just one young person with my words, I would continue to write and publish for the rest of my life, with little concern over whether I made a buck at it or not.

On November 2nd, 1972 ... I walked out of the Chillicothe Correctional Institute into the free world. I was on parole.

If I had entertained the notion that there'd be a brass band waiting, or that society would accept me back with open arms, I would have been a fool. There are many people who simply are not convinced that convicts should be released on parole. "Lock 'em up and throw the key away" is their response to most of the problems of crime and correction. Fortunately, the cost of imprisonment is so unrealistically high that the parole authorities are pressured into releasing more and more men on parole. This not only relieves an overcrowded prison system—but it gives the offender an opportunity to "work his way back" into society.

The pressures and problems of the ex-convict can be monumental. With fifty dollars in his pocket, he must find a place to live, pay for his food, and try to keep himself solvent until he gets a job and a paycheck. If this sounds like an impossible task, it often is. And it is the primary reason why so many ex-

convicts return to crime so quickly. It is simply un-
realistic to expect an unattached male in a modern
world to live for three or four months on fifty dollars.
On top of this, the ex-con is given one suit of clothing
when he leaves prison. What is he to wear to work if
he gets a job? The suit and shirt and tie the prison
gave him?

In my own case, I fared better since my writing
had earned me a small nest egg which accumulated
during my prison days. In spite of this I still found the
going tough for the first six months.

Luckily, I had contacts in the broadcasting indus-
try and I landed a job as Public Relations Director of
the Columbia School of Broadcasting. Jim Uglum, the
owner, had been a personal friend of mine back in
my early radio days in Missoula, Montana, and he was
willing and eager to give me a chance to work.

In the meantime, I continue to work, to write, and
to try to function as a responsible, mature free man.
I have made many new friends in Cincinnati, Ohio,
where I now make my home.

The men who live at the L. B. Harrison Club, a
private men's residence club in Cincinnati, have accepted me openly and honestly. I have been able to
have meaningful and warm relationships with many
of the residents. Charlie Shear, the manager of the
club has gone out of his way to be of help, paving the
way for my acceptance in and out of the club.

One of the bright spots in my parole days was
meeting Jack Harrington, his wife Sandy, and their
children. Jack is the director for this area of a remarkable group of businessmen called "Man-to-Man Associates." These ordinary citizens offer the hand of

friendship to individual convicts still in prison and help pave their way when they get out by aiding them in their search for jobs and a place to stay. The most important thing they give their "convict friend" is real interest and warm concern. The record of this outstanding group of dedicated citizens is impressive and they are having deserved growth throughout the nation.

Many idealistic people, like Francis Dale, Publisher of the "Cincinnati Enquirer," simply refuse to believe that there are men and women who should be "born to lose." By working hard through such organizations as the National Council on Crime and Delinquency, as well as local prison and jail reform groups, these people translate their ideals into action.

I can only thank God that there are still people in the world who are willing to take one more chance on the miserable and most damaged of society's rejects. I have benefited from that concern. Most importantly I have developed a feeling of trust and responsibility toward these people.

I am grateful that the State of Ohio sees fit to trust me on parole. I am determined to "make it."

But most importantly, I have made a personal commitment to see to it that I do not let my many friends down. In so doing, I will not let myself down. Far too many people would be deeply hurt and disappointed if I were to fall again. I accept this tremendous burden. It is a burden of love.

Did I deserve help? Probably not. But I am glad that there are so many unsung and unmentioned decent people in and out of the prison system who

"On November 2, 1972 . . . I walked out of the Chillicothe Correctional Institute into a free world. . . . If I had entertained the notion that there'd be a brass band waiting, or that society would accept me back with open arms, I would have been a fool."

did offer me their friendship, trust, and help. To them, my "making it" will be a monument we can share. It is possible to change one who is "born to lose" into one who can "make it."

It seems to me that as long as we have faith in the ability of one errant human being to change or to reform, then there is great hope for all humans as a great society.

My parole will end on November 2nd, 1973.* At that time my civil rights will be restored and I will be a free man in every way. There will be one exception. I will still . . . and always be . . . an ex-convict. There is no way under existing statutes to erase that blemish upon my life.

But there will be a striking change. I will no longer think and act like an outsider. I will share the burden of living in a group in my city, state, and nation.

I will never completely belong. But I will have "made it" enough to stay straight.

My burning hope for the remainder of my life will be to share my criminal and prison experiences with young people everywhere in the hope that they can get some insights into their own feelings.

Every person born has worth. It has taken me forty-five years to find my own value.

Now I want to help others to find their own worth.

The fight is just beginning.

---

*Since this book has gone to press, Lou Torok has been officially released from parole and is now on his own.

Life in Prison

In Harper Lee's novel *To Kill a Mockingbird* the character Atticus Finch explains to his eleven year old son, Jem, that to understand another person's feelings "You have to crawl right inside the other man's skin and walk around." Someone who has not been inside a prison, never served a sentence as a convict, cannot understand what it is like to lose freedom, dignity and human rights. I am going to try to tell you something about what it feels like to be in prison.

In our country today, there are many types of prisons. There are prisons where men are cooped up four

29

to a cage for 24 hours a day without sunlight, fresh air or exercise. Many of these prisoners go insane after a while. In more modern prisons, convicts have more freedom within the walls to go to and from their meals and prison jobs. After the evening meal, such convicts usually return to the cells or dormitories where they stay at night and over weekends. Then there is a new kind of prison which is becoming more common as the public learns that it is possible for convicts to be rehabilitated and become good citizens. Such prisons have only a fence around them and a minimum of armed guards. Most of the convicts live in large, open dormitories, get plenty of fresh air and exercise and much more personal freedom within the prison. However, these men are still in prison; they cannot go home or go out at night or on weekends.

There are men in prison who were serving time before you were born and who will still be there when you are grown up. When the judge convicted me to a prison sentence of from one to ten years, it made me stop and think whether or not I could actually stand up to that long a sentence. Ten years is a long time. If you want to understand how much time it is, try to think about what ten years means in your own life. Think back ten years. How old were you? Can you even remember that far back? How old will you be ten years from now? Where will you be living then, what will you be doing? You might even be married and have children of your own. I want you to try to understand what a terrible price to pay for any crime a long prison sentence really is.

But there are other punishments worse than just

"... inmates in some institutions are treated more like animals in a zoo than like human beings."

being in prison. The convict must live his life without freedom of movement, privacy or normal companionship and with all kinds of restrictions and regulations. He may be subjected to physical abuse and this in turn may seem like minor punishment compared to the loneliness and boredom and lack of human contact he experiences day after day and year after year in prison. Some maximum security prisons crowd convicts into cramped cells all day and all night. When the men go to meals, work or church, they must march in military formation. If a man steps out of line or talks he will be severely punished. Most prisons have a lot of petty rules designed to force the convict to conform. Regulations like these help to make prison life seem like hell on earth. Many convicts feel that not only have they lost their civil rights but their membership in the human race as well. Although convicts in newer institutions may be treated more humanely, it is not uncommon to find them living in filth, degeneracy and brutality beyond words in many prisons today. It could be said that the inmates in some institutions are treated more like animals in a zoo than like human beings.

At the Ohio Penitentiary, when I was there, we lived four to a cell. There was just one 40-watt light bulb for the four of us to read by. The space was so cramped that only one man could walk between the bunks at a time. The toilet was in a corner of the cell and there was no privacy when one of us wanted to use it. A single tap of putrid, cold water had to serve for drinking, washing, shaving and also for washing our clothes. The prison did not launder any underclothing and it was necessary for nearly 2000 men to wash their underclothes in cold water in their cells if they wanted to keep clean. Of course, many men simply did not wash their clothes and the resulting stench, under conditions where we were living so close together, was unbelievable.

To a man in prison, mealtime becomes abnormally important, constituting almost the only acceptable event in his life. Convicts look forward eagerly to their meals and if the food is spoiled or improperly prepared, trouble may ensue. As a rule, prisons are not known for the quality of their cuisine. The food is usually tasteless, poorly balanced and the cheapest available on the market. True, at the modern prisons, like the Chillicothe Correctional Institute where I was incarcerated the food is of fair quality and we were lucky to be able to join whomever we pleased at small four-man tables. This is quite unlike the conditions existing in the majority of prison dining rooms, where the men sit at long narrow tables, crowded together like sardines, and given only a few minutes to eat in absolute silence. Under these conditions, perhaps you can understand why most prison riots and trouble originate in the dining room?

Putting convicts who break prison rules on short rations is a typical punishment. Prisoners in maximum security prisons are punished with what is called "solitary confinement." To the convicts, solitary is known as the "hole." Here convicts are given a bare minimum of food to keep them going and are kept locked up in dark cells without a mattress or clean bedding on which to sleep. In some prisons their clothes are taken away and they are kept naked. Prison officials today often refer to this type of treatment as "correctional detention." Whatever it is called, it dehumanizes men.

There are approximately 3,000 jails and prisons in the United States which house over 3½ million prisoners at the latest count. In many of these prisons, the conditions are very crowded and there are not enough jobs to keep the inmates busy. In these prisons, the men may just sit around all day long and stare at the walls or at each other. If they stay in their cells, they may lie on their bunks all day in utter boredom and stagnation. This inertia can go on year after year. Are you surprised that many of these men will not be able to hold down a regular job when they are released? Those of them who have no job skill will probably return to prison.

The convict who has been placed in a prison which has a really worthwhile work and study program may consider himself fortunate indeed. There are experiments on hand to allow screened convicts to go to work outside the prison every day, returning to their cells at night. Some men are even permitted to attend special trade schools and colleges nearby. Where such programs have been implemented, they have proved very effective. Less than 10 per cent of the convicts in these programs have broken trust. But few programs of this sort are available.

In Chillicothe Correctional Institute, my job was that of chief clerk for the Medical Director of the prison hospital. My work was to answer the phone, fill out forms and type letters and memoranda for the doctor in charge. I enjoyed my job especially because it brought me into daily contact with civilian workers inside the prison. Their relaxed attitudes greatly helped in my eventual rehabilitation. I formed friendships with these people which would not ordinarily have been possible inside prison.

Some prisoners work in industrial shops such as the tobacco factory where tobacco products are processed for other prisons; in the print shop, furniture factory, bakery, butcher shop, power plant, etc. Other inmates cook and serve our food or help keep the prison clean. There are even prisons, especially

Mr. Torok notes that many prisoners "lie on their bunks all day in utter boredom and stagnation;" but he suggests an alternative —prison employment. At Chillicothe Correctional Institute he worked as chief clerk for the Medical Director of the prison hospital. That position brought him into daily contact with civilian workers, which he feels was instrumental in his eventual rehabilitation.

in New England, which allow convicts to operate small businesses inside the facility.

Many years ago, the labor of convicts was sold to the highest bidders among local farmers and quarry owners. Thus the convict was forced into a form of slave labor. This practice has largely been discontinued. Today, most convicts who work in prison at a job are paid a small token wage. In the State of Ohio, for instance, convicts earn about 10 dollars a month. Six dollars of that money serves as credit in the prison store where coffee, candy, cigarettes, toilet articles or other permitted articles can be sold. Four dollars is put into a special "going home" fund for the prisoner's use on release or on parole. Some prisoners are even able to send small amounts of money home to poor families.

Most states have far to go before they have brought prison job-training programs to a level where they are constructively helping the men behind bars. As I have told you, many prisons do not have enough work to keep most of the prisoners occupied. The chief problem of prison life being boredom and loneliness, it sometimes happens that an inmate who just sits around all day with nothing to occupy himself goes "stir-crazy" (prison slang for going mad).

The convict in prison feels alone, isolated, waiting day after day for the end of a sentence which seems as if it will never come. He talks with the same people day after day. Opportunities for diversion, entertainment and relaxation are limited. The unchanging scene is boring to the point of pain. Those prisoners who have a hobby, can play a musical instrument, paint, or write, have an advantage over the inmates who do not have these resources to help occupy and absorb them. My writing gave me great personal satisfaction. With the lifting of censorship on incoming and outgoing mail within the Ohio prison system in my last few years of imprisonment there, I found myself communicating with an increasing number of people, young people especially, who wrote to me concerning the articles and stories I had begun to write about prison conditions and convict problems. The history of literature is filled with examples of writers who started to write while in prison. Convicts who have a great deal of time to serve should be encouraged to write and read as much as possible.

There are prisons which do not permit the inmates to have any reading materials other than a Bible. In some states it is compulsory for convicts to be provided with a Bible to read when alone in the cells. Today, more enlightened institutions have large, well-stocked libraries for the use of the inmates. The majority of the men in prison probably prefer the sort of spicy, popular fiction that can be found displayed in drug stores. Other convicts have little or no use for books, use them as missiles or destroy them without thought for fellow inmates. Therefore most books in the average prison library will be paperbacks or cheap editions of popular best-selling novels. Many convicts however respect books and ideas. Convicts in the more liberal penitentiaries are able to subscribe to a wide variety of newspapers and magazines. I would imagine that almost every magazine published in this country will be found in its jails.

"My writing gave me great personal satisfaction. ... I found myself communicating with an increasing number of people, young people especially, who wrote to me concerning the articles and stories I had begun to write about prison conditions and convict problems."

I have seen unlikely looking convicts poring over copies of, for instance, "Scientific American" or "Fortune Magazine."

Another way in which some convicts combat the boredom of prison life is to keep pets. Convicts in maximum security prisons have been known to adopt unusual pets such as cockroaches, even training them to perform tricks for their entertainment. Other inmates have captured mice and raised whole generations of them. Many convicts in prisons all round the country are allowed to keep canaries in cages in their cells and dormitories. When I was in prison in Maine, the lifers were allowed their choice of pet. Some had monkeys, one even bought an alligator by mail, others kept parrots in their cells. But after a while, most pets just disappeared as the men began to observe that the animals did not thrive in the prison atmosphere and so they released them. One lifer for instance had a beautiful little dog he named "Martini." The dog gradually became lethargic and one day the convict let a guard take his pet home for the weekend. When the prisoner heard how happy his dog was outside the prison walls, he did not have the heart to take it back. He realized, with greater awareness than society, that neither animals nor men can bear to be caged.

When I was a 17-year-old sailor, home on leave from the Navy, I visited the Ohio Penitentiary, out of curiosity, on a guided tour. I saw the cells where the men lived inside the high stone walls. I actually saw the electric chair. At the time that seemed like quite a thrill. The entire experience might have been meaningless to me had I not entered the kitchen area and seen a large, ugly convict, stripped to the waist and sweating like a horse, who was carving meat for the evening meal with a large, sharp butcher knife. I will never forget the image of hatred he conveyed to me. I vowed never to invade the privacy of convicts again. Little did I think that some day I too would be viewed, like a monkey in a cage, by anyone who had the price of admission. Many inmates of prisons do feel like caged animals on display. Intelligent prison administrators are careful not to parade visitors through the prison on guided tours. Visitors of this sort are more likely to come individually or in small groups. Sometimes a large group is allowed inside to attend some activity like a concert, sporting event or religious service; but in these cases they are sharing an experience with the convicts.

While some penologists are beginning to experiment with limited weekend passes and with work and study furloughs for well-behaved convicts, such opportunities for normal living conditions are extremely rare. Above all, the unfulfilled sexual urges of men who have been in prison for long periods of time without women, without their normal sexual outlets, can be explosively dangerous. Prison life is brutally indifferent and cold. I have seen men bite a pillow in the night and cry out. A young man's urge for sexual companionship is blocked by the artificial prison isolation. No matter how hard the uninitiated man may try to avoid it, he is going to hear and learn a great deal about homosexuality. He may be confronted by it in a brutal way. It is the rare convict who will never engage in homosexual acts. For one sort of convict, the love and tenderness he seeks from

other inmates will enable him to retain his mental
and emotional balance and to continue to function as
a human being. But the reality of much prison sex is
terror. This is especially true where young boys are
involved. "They'll be lined up waiting for you boy.
You'll be gang raped like a girl. The old cons like 'em
young like you."

An old, bearded convict, snickering through a
toothless grin, was taunting a young prisoner spending his first night in jail. For his part, the teenager
was stunned. His mouth hung open. His bravado
failed him and he did not know how to keep up a
"tough" front. In the free world, out on the street,
with his gang, he could bluff his way through anything, almost. Here he was alone, outnumbered, de-
fenseless against the older, more experienced and
assaultive convicts with whom he would be living
and sleeping from now on. He would be treated like
a girl because he was young and soft. He would have
to submit. This young rebel was beginning to have
serious doubts about his choice for a life of crime but
it was too late: the circle of convicts was narrowing,
moving in for another gang rape.

The official prison attitude towards homosexuality
is a mixed one. It is recognized as a serious problem
but one that must be tolerated in order to avoid serious trouble. Many officials choose to ignore the issue,
to feign surprise when asked and inquire innocently
"What homosexuality?" A convict with privileged
status and influence can get the guards and officials
to "look the other way." If he has enough pull he can
get away with homosexual conduct. Thus, among the
"right" people, homosexuality in prison is condoned.

Marriage between convicts is not unknown. In some prisons a wedding ceremony can be arranged, complete with ring, blushing bride and proud family. Divorce can be arranged in the same fashion when either party is unfaithful. And in the prison world of promiscuity, this can be rather frequent.

For other convicts, those without the necessary pull, homosexual acts will be punished. In some prisons those caught will be thrown into the hole and denied privileges for long periods of time. The prison authorities might add a further punishment by sending a letter to the families of prisoners involved, informing them that their husband, father or son has been caught in a homosexual act. Thus convicts are robbed of their sexual dignity.

Many convicts feel they are being punished endlessly for every mistake they ever committed and that they will never be free again. There is an expression "doing time on the installment plan." This refers to those convicts who as soon as they finish one prison sentence and go out on parole commit some crime which brings them right back to the place they claim to hate so much. One such man told me his story. He seemed intelligent but had such an intense hatred of policemen that as soon as he saw one he would feel an uncontrollable urge to hit him. Naturally, the police were not very sympathetic to this man's hang-up and so he continued to go back into prison over and over again.

He had spent his childhood in a small town in Maine. His family was poor and they lived in the wrong part of town. The small ragged child would wander into the better parts of town, and the local police, finding him, would beat him up and send him scuttling back home. As he grew up, he developed a deep and lasting hatred for all people in authority, teachers for instance, as well as policemen, and this hatred included everyone in uniform, even bus drivers. His reaction to the damage done him as an impressionable young child had been a violent one and his way of dealing with it was by the use of violence. A lot of people who end up in prison have learned to hate authority figures in a similar way. It is a syndrome from which many convicts cannot escape.

Our prisons are filled with men and women who were abused as young children. Such people need a great deal of help. Convicts should be given a chance to work their way back into society. While reforms are gradually taking place in the correctional systems the rate of change is far too slow.

Looking Back

~~~~~~

I remember that I was nine years old when I first had an overwhelming desire to steal. As a child I was an orphan and spent many years in places which seemed frighteningly lonely. I didn't have anyone to buy me things like ice cream and candy so I thought I'd just take care of that problem the best way I could. I found that the only way I'd get anything was by stealing it.

I was a ward of the juvenile court; that is, the juvenile court judge was acting as my legal father because I had no parents. At the time, I did not understand this. Nobody bothered to explain it to me. I thought the judge was in charge of me because I had done something wrong. As a result, even as a small child, I thought of myself as a criminal and no good. Since I believed I was being treated like a criminal, I tried to oblige those in charge of me by acting like one. I was raised in an orphanage, in foster homes and in a boys' school. By today's standards, these places were really strict. I still have some scars on my body from the rough treatment I received as a dependent child. It was common to be beaten and abused in many ways by those in authority. Most of the criminal behavior I learned, I learned in those places, many of which, interestingly enough, still exist. I hope that they will have changed their ways.

I learned early in life that I could lie, cheat, steal and do almost anything I wanted as long as I presented a clean face and a bright smile to the people who raised me. It was always so easy to con them. If I could isolate a single factor which, I believe, eventually brought about my three prison sentences, it was the feeling I had as a child that I was smarter than my teachers and those who raised me. It seemed that they were always too busy, that they didn't have time for the real needs of any child. I learned to cheat and to steal and to disobey those in authority because I felt that they didn't care about me. I felt that the rules and orders didn't apply to me.

I used to wonder if I was influenced by bad company as so many people have suggested. Actually, I can easily answer that question. I was the bad company everybody worries about. This is a terrible thing to have to admit after all these years. But I would like you to understand that children who are bad influences on others do not usually realize it at the time. As I look back on my childhood in institutions, I see that at various times I was both leader and follower, although I tended to be more often a leader. I had a gang of two other boys with whom I shared many illicit adventures. When we got into trouble they usually blamed me for whatever we had done so I guess this made me their leader. But I often remember telling my teachers that it wasn't my fault if these friends did anything I told them to do. I guess I was lying to my teacher. I am sure now that I led my friends astray and that I did it willingly. There was so little fun in our lives in those bleak days that we would do practically anything to break the monotony and boredom—and we did do some fairly weird things.

I remember being thrown out of school a dozen times or more. But since there was no other school to which my friends or I could be sent, we always got taken back. Of course I took maximum advantage of this fact. I must have been a terrible problem. I don't know how any of my teachers could possibly have liked me. However, there was one teacher once who seemed to understand and love me. I shall always admire and respect that teacher who today is teaching Arab children in the Jordanian desert. A child is lucky if he can find a special teacher who cares about him when no one else seems to. A child without love and affection will do almost anything to attract attention to himself, even if all he gains is a beating. Discipline makes him a rebel which brings him the attention he craves.

Like many criminals, I thought I could be a law

unto myself. I was independent and very self-willed. I was not willing to listen to the advice or suggestions of other people. This is a mistake which many criminals make: they feel that the laws and rules of society are a joke, that they are made only for other people. Often I am asked if I ever stopped to think that I might be caught committing a crime or if I ever considered the penalties. I must be honest and answer this question with a definite *no*. Like most criminals I was very egotistical and could not believe that I would ever be caught because I was smarter than the police and everyone else. After all, this is part of the reason why I had turned to crime in the first place.

I have never been sentenced to the workhouse or the county jail. The very first time I was caught breaking the law, I was sent straight to San Quentin. I started young and I started right at the top of the prison ladder. I do not believe that this would happen today. But it is already too late to erase the scars that have been left on me by such careless indifference on the part of the authorities. I graduated from San Quentin at 21.

I have never robbed anyone with a knife or gun. I don't believe that I would ever willingly harm another person physically. I have been a burglar and I have also embezzled money from my employer. I told myself that I only wanted to steal the money to do the things which I felt I was entitled to do because I had never had the things I had wanted as a child. I believed I had a right to the money which I stole. I could not break all the bad habits I had learned as a child when I became a man. Even later, when I was

a husband and the father of a son, I found myself
stealing out of habit. After three prison sentences I
am finally learning to control my behaviour, to alter
the habits of a lifetime.

My life has been complex and there are many
things that have contributed to my lingering feelings
of insecurity, of being unwanted, of not belonging.
Many children raised in institutions and foster homes
end up as adults with similarly negative feelings. It is
not easy for the adults who raise such children to do
the job adequately. It takes heroic amounts of love,
real concern, patience and understanding to help a
child such as I was to overcome those deep feelings
of unworthiness. Anything less than total commitment will fail as it did with me and thousands of
others just like me.

As I grew older, I discovered that I had been the
child of parents who had been too poor to take care
of me. I found out that I had a brother and a sister.
I have since become close to both of them although
I am afraid at times that they may feel quite ashamed
of me. They were more fortunate than I was as they
were raised by relatives. The court had assumed responsibility for me and I was the only one who had
been sent to an orphanage.

In my teens I enlisted in the Navy. I served in the
South Pacific. At one time I was even a guard over
Japanese prisoners-of-war in an American prison
camp on the island of Guam. It is somewhat ironic to
think that not long after that I myself would be a
prisoner. My Navy days paid off for me because I
decided not to waste my time. I enrolled in high
school and college courses and while other sailors

were shooting dice and playing poker, I was studying. When I returned home I got my high school diploma. After I got out of San Quentin I spent practically fourteen years attending a variety of night colleges whenever I was in the mood. In this way I got a patchwork education in the wide variety of things that interest me.

However, there were difficult problems in my civilian life which I felt unable to solve. There were domestic conflicts.My wife discovered I was an ex-convict and divorced me. Then she remarried and went to live in Denmark taking our son with her. After that, the world as I knew it came to an abrupt end.Whatever happened subsequently seems unimportant now, and in fact, I find it hard to believe that it actually happened. But time is a miraculous healer. Slowly over the years that followed my personal loss, I have recovered control of my own life. I feel now that I can suffer personally the tragedies of other human beings having myself touched bottom. It is my hope to interpret and report on the causes and solutions to these tragedies to those interested enough to read what I write. I want to make my stretches of time in prison serve some humane objective and to have some meaning other than just so many marks on the calendar.

When I was first in prison, it was easy for me to escape the harsh realities of daily life by daydreaming. I did not try to face up to the truth about the awful conditions or about why I was there. But as time went on, I found it becoming increasingly helpful to try and face life in prison as it really was. I had to have a plan for the future. This eventually

Lou at work in his cell. Looming in the foreground, his type-writer stands as a symbol of rehabilitation for the "Convict Writer."

launched me on a career as a convict writer. Writing gave me a chance to express the deep creative urge which I believe lies dormant in most of us. It also gave me an outlet for my restless energies in prison. In a way, writing was an escape from the otherwise drab and oppressive daily grind. I have tried to apply intelligence and insight to my writing and I am pleased when someone writes to me to tell me that he understands exactly what I mean by something that I have written. Actually, if intelligence and insight work correctly, people would be unlikely to end up, as I have, in prison. Whatever insights I have obtained have been the result of long and painful examination and soul-searching which for me started after I entered prison.

What Causes Crime

~~~~~~

   In the 19th Century, the theories of a famous phrenologist, (phrenology being the scientific study of the bumps on one's head) that the shape of a person's head was the best indication of criminality, were taken very seriously. A much more recent theory attempts to prove that unusual body chemistry, in the form of an extra chromosome, in certain tall adult males causes their criminal behavior. Later research has questioned this theory but other hypotheses, more bizarre perhaps, will no doubt be forthcoming as certain social scientists continue to research their pet theories about the causes and

cures of crime. Everyone wants to find a simple formula by which to predict criminal tendencies, even
in small babies.

Of course there is no simple answer to such an
extremely complex human and social problem. Any
solution to the apparent increase in violence and lawlessness can come only with the application of individual solutions to individual problems. Criminal
behavior should be studied on an individual, not a
mass basis. There is no single cause of crime just as
there is no single cause of blindness.

Most of the crimes that are committed each year
involve property. The criminal steals money, a car or
some tangible property that has a saleable value.
Some psychologists today feel that acquisitive crime,
as this sort of crime is called, is a reflection of very
deep social problems rather than isolated but persis-
tent aggressive and antisocial acts.

You have heard this said before, but my opinion is
that one of the biggest causes of crime today is the
loosening of the bonds of morality in our society.
There is widespread corruption in high places; graft,
bribery, extortion, influence-peddling can assume
the form of multi-million dollar conspiracies by powerful people and companies against other large cor-
porations and the Government. There is a double
standard which makes it possible for a citizen with
influential friends to acquire huge assets in public
funds while the social failure from the ghetto will be
punished severely if he tries to pull off some minor
illegal act in order to get a few bucks to feed a hungry
family. Less than 10 per cent of all criminals are ever
caught in the United States. The greatest number of

criminals are very successful and can afford high-priced lawyers to help them avoid jail even if they are caught. Most convicts in prison resent this double standard. They resent a system which righteously punishes them while tolerating a supposedly honest fellow citizen who would stoop to rob from a blind man.

A lot of young people, as they begin to break away from the controls of their family, school, church and familiar neighborhood groups, find that they cannot respect the beliefs and teachings of older people who do not practice what they preach. Another source of confusion and irritation is the existence of laws that are unenforceable or even ridiculous by the standards of modern society. I am always impressed however by the large numbers of teenagers who live good, happy and law-abiding lives despite all the problems of growing up. A lot of petty crime is committed by young people just looking for some fun who will soon outgrow this need for thrills and excitement. They do not consider that many of the things they do for fun may be illegal. For instance, car stealing; many kids think that when they are bored and restless its really fun, and easy, to go out and pick up a car to go joyriding. Car stealing, shoplifting, taking dope may seem like fun. The hard part comes with the long prison sentence, with the best part of your life to be lived behind bars. There is another group of mostly young people however who commit crimes of violence; those who are under the influence of hard drugs and need money to support an expensive habit. Many young people today are not willing to exercise control over their feelings and urges or to ask if by doing their own thing they will hurt other people.

With the basic immorality that spawns crime comes the widespread lack of respect for the law among ordinary citizens. In one year alone, bank robbers hauled off ten million dollars in 1,500 separate robberies. These daring holdups were the deliberate and desperate acts of criminals. In the same year, American businessmen lost five hundred million dollars from white collar crime, the so-called petty thievery committed by customers and employees. These white-collar crimes were the surreptitious acts of supposedly honest citizens.

The typical prison inmate is confused and bitter over the steady barrage of immorality and disrespect for law and order which streams in on him over his radio earphones and which he reads in the daily newspapers. Most convicts do not understand why they should be in prison with so much lawlessness going on outside the prison walls. They realize that they have been forced to pay dearly for their acts while the double standard in operation in the free world permits the supposedly honest square johns to rob an employer or local merchant at will.

White-collar crime is the term used to describe the petty thievery which is indulged in each day by millions of Americans when they steal a towel or spoon from a hotel or take a pen or box of paperclips from an employer. White-collar crime is the result of the cancer-like attitude that tolerates and encourages deception and thievery based on the rationale—"I really have it coming to me." This attitude might arise from a deep-rooted feeling of victimization, real or imagined; outrage, on the part of an employee for instance who feels that his employer does not pay a fair living wage; anger against a supermarket or store that charges such high prices that the customer feels justified in stealing something and beating the owner at his own game.

It seems to me that neither free citizens nor convicts can continue any longer to be blasé towards public and private violations of trust. We should not close our eyes and look the other way when we notice white-collar crime in action. As long as we choose to tolerate and ignore certain things we will continue to have more crime in our society.

Most of the convicts I have met in prison were there because nobody cared enough about them when they were kids or took the time to tell them right from wrong. Once in prison, the convict is far more likely to be dehumanized by his treatment there than to be turned into a well-adjusted law-abiding citizen. Also, by keeping convicts exclusively in the company of other criminals we can only perpetuate a self-defeating system of crime and criminal education.

There are people who believe that imprisoning criminals for a long time actually contributes to our growing crime rate. The public knows very little about prisons or the system that operates in them. No prison can legally hold a convict beyond the term of his sentence. Most convicts are paroled before the completion of their term. At the present time, our prison system is turning out not good citizens but mad dogs. If convicts were treated with dignity and respect, the case might be different, but prisoners who have been treated brutally and without humanity return to the community as aggressors. True rehabilitation and correction would be productive for the community at large as well as for the convict to whom human dignity would thus be restored. Punishment is wastefully expensive. Of the entire prison population of the United States today, at least 90 per cent do not need intensive prison care or treatment. Leaving aside the psychotic criminal who should be in a hospital or the social deviant who could be in a treatment center, most prisoners are potentially more harmful to themselves than others. But we continue to support the prison system simply because we have always done it this way. Non-violent criminals could be trained to redirect their antisocial attitudes and given useful job-training to help them fulfill their desire for achievement and provide the material things they want without resorting to crime. Crime, which, looked at one way, is really just behavior which takes unfair advantage of other people, will only stop when all people genuinely start to care about one another.

Meanwhile, the man who ends up in prison is often not only a criminal but a failure at crime as well. It has been my observation that crime is often an individual's response to an intolerable personal problem. Much crime is committed by disadvantaged people who are trying to fulfill their unmet social, cultural or economic needs through the short-cut way of crime. A study of the convicts in any prison will show that most of them share similar patterns of disadvantage: most of them lack basic education; are from backgrounds lacking in economic security and cultural

The prison uniform, circa 1914

opportunities, and were unable to hold down the most elementary badly-paying job. Is it surprising that so many of these criminals have a low opinion of themselves? How can people who are failures in so many areas of life have any pride or dignity or wish to live by the standards of a community to which they do not belong?

Crime is as old as civilization itself. If you think about it, crime is actually the behavior of a few people which is disapproved of by the majority. After all, habits and customs vary from country to country. What may be thought of as normal behavior in one place may be considered criminal in another.

Who is a Criminal?

What are criminals really like? To answer that question, you must, to begin with, eliminate from your mind every stereotyped conception you may have held since childhood. Movies, novels, newspapers and television often romanticize criminals. Children playing in the streets and parks still play that favorite game—"Bang, bang! I gotcha. . . . you're dead!" as they shoot their playmates with toy guns. It is possible to grow up retaining that same childhood view of crime as a game played by criminals. Actually, a criminal is usually just an ordinary person who happens to have bigger social problems.

Prisons are filled with people who could not keep their hands off the property of others. Unfortunately, most of the people who wind up in prison for theft learned to steal as children. Psychologists have suggested that stealing may be the sign of deeper underlying problems. The thief often does not know why he feels compelled to steal from other people. Most children seem to know that stealing is wrong but many of them are powerless to stop themselves. As mentioned earlier, we really know very little about the causes of criminal behavior.

Many children embark upon a life of crime by taking small, insignificant things from their parents. Usually these are articles of little or no value which the child thinks will not even be missed. Gradually, he experiments with taking things from people outside the family circle. This is exciting, especially if he doesn't get caught at it. Later on perhaps he expands into stealing from the neighborhood store, and gets away with it. Upon questioning children have often said that they steal as much or more for the thrill of it as for the things they steal. Among the numerous convicted thieves are those who began their careers as child thieves, taking things in stores for a dare or to be one of the gang. To prove their courage and skill to classmates who had challenged them to shoplift was far more important than the act itself. At first it was fun. Then it became a way for the child to get anything that he wanted without paying. The truth is that once a child begins to enjoy stealing just for the fun of it, he is well on his way to prison.

Many teenage shoplifters graduate to car theft. After that it is car stripping and selling the parts for

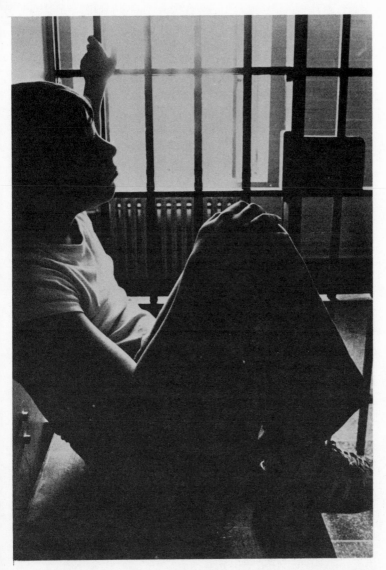

It is scenes like this that Mr. Torok is striving to prevent: "If I thought I could reach just one young person with my words, I would continue to write and publish for the rest of my life, with little concern over whether I made a buck at it or not."

money. The next step for the apprentice thief is big-time crime, like armed robbery. Some young people are caught early on for such seemingly innocent crimes as shoplifting and car-borrowing and they are sent to the reformatory. It is here that they will meet older and more sophisticated criminals who will teach them a great deal about crime. They will learn many new tricks before they are twenty-one. They may be taught how to rob banks, break into safes, how to enter and leave a store or private home without being discovered by the owner. They learn many criminal skills that an ordinary child would never learn. The reformatory, more than anything else, is a school of crime.

Perhaps ordinary citizens may find it hard to understand why the criminal will not settle down and work at a regular job like other people. The answer to that is that most criminals are not trained in anything else but crime. Many thieves are released from reformatories and really try to go straight. But they soon find that the only thing they know how to do is steal. Instead of teaching him a useful trade, the reformatory or prison turned him from an amateur into a professional criminal. If he is caught by the police again, because he has a prison record he will quickly be sent back to jail. The police, the courts, other citizens, all regard him now as a hardened criminal. Many youngsters have been in and out of prisons and reformatories several times before they have even turned twenty-one.

I have received several letters from young people asking me if I broke the law out of desperation or just for kicks. To tell the truth, many people who break the law are unaware that their behavior is criminal. Often the convict cannot understand why he is in prison. He feels that if he doesn't agree with or respect a certain law he is entitled to violate it. I am asked if I ever stopped to consider that I might be caught committing a crime or if I thought about the possible consequences. As I have explained before, I believed that I would not be caught because I was smarter than the cops. The fact is that the majority of criminals do not get caught. The only sort of criminals you hear about are the ones who end up in jail, the unsuccessful ones, that is. Successful criminals can afford to maintain a respectable front and with the help of expensive lawyers can avoid a lengthy prison sentence in the unlikely event that they are caught.

The convicted criminals are, therefore, in most cases failures. Nearly half the inmates of jails have serious psychological or personality problems. Over 40 percent have one or more physical disability in addition to social problems. It is nearly impossible for such people to get along with others or to live and compete in the job market of our dynamic society. Many disabled and deformed men turn to crime as a way of getting what they want and need. The average, law-abiding citizen works hard to raise a family without thinking too much about why or how he does it. But what about a one-armed man? What about a man with a facial deformity like a hair-lip or some grotesque physical abnormality which makes it difficult for him to meet the public? Or a person with a serious emotional problem? Most of us think nothing about just walking down the street or going to the store. A person with a physical disability is unable, or feels unable, to do that. We admire a beautiful sunset. The person with partial vision will never share our joy. The man with a serious hearing loss cannot enjoy television as we can, much less hold down a job. Many disabled and deformed people in prison feel inferior. Can you blame them for turning to crime? A great number of convicts have social or psychological handicaps that keep them from effectively working with other people. For instance, a large number of prison inmates cannot even read or write.

For many of these unfortunate persons, prison is a way for them to get the care and attention they need. Many of them are not sophisticated enough to seek out proper solutions or to ask for help through the available channels. They need help. But few hospitals will take them. They may have no money. Welfare agencies may not be interested in their cases; perhaps they have not lived in the area long enough. They don't qualify for social security or workmens' compensation. They have never had enough money together at one time to be able to afford any insurance. Without money, insurance or eligibility for social programs they are unable to get help anywhere. So they take the only way out for them and commit a crime for which they will be sent to prison.

There is a myth that convicts are tough. Mental toughness and self-discipline are qualities that would help any man to serve his prison sentence more easily. Convicts call it "doing easy time." But most convicts have neither quality. Most of the so-called physical toughs are the very first to crack under pressure. You can usually tell where they are in prison by their constant complaining.

Another common erroneous myth is that convicts are loyal to one another. Unfortunately, this is not the case. Our prisons are filled with convicts who eagerly curry favor with the prison administrators by selling them information about their fellow inmates in exchange for privileges. They will betray their best friends if neccessary. These are the people who are sorry they committed criminal acts, not because they might have hurt someone but because they got caught. They think that the rules of society don't apply to them and that crime is just a short-cut to a desired goal. Few of these criminals are honest either intellectually or emotionally. If you believe that convicts are loyal to each other, you should spend a few hours in any prison observing the affection-seeking maneuvers and the rationalizations of those desperately lonely men who want to be loved, understood and accepted but who are not capable of giving anything in return and who are utterly self-centered.

Lest I paint a totally negative portrait let me say that there is another side to these men. I have seen dedication, loyalty, affection, trust, kindness and self-sacrifice from the most unlikely sources. I have also met some extremely interesting people in prison.

To help you to understand the typical kind of social failure who ends up in prison, I'd like to tell you the story of a convict I once knew. Let's call him Jerry. Jerry is a forty-three year old man in prison for the rape of a seventeen year old girl. Under the old laws of our frontier justice days, Jerry might have been taken out and hung from the nearest strong tree. This rough sort of justice was believed to help solve society's problems. It certainly ended the criminal's problems. The main problem that contributed to Jerry's downfall was a lack of early parental care and interest. His family was very poor, although if it had been rich the story might have been the same. Jerry hung around with a group of tough neighborhood boys. He soon ended up in the hands of the juvenile officials. They put Jerry in a jail cell, not, they said, to punish him, but "for his own good." But Jerry knew they were lying, he knew they didn't really care what happened to him. Thus the seeds of a lifetime of bitterness were sewn into his young mind.

It's a miracle he ever made it to manhood. He always seemed to want more out of life than the other kids. He managed to survive the bleak years in the reformatory where he was sent when his foster family no longer wanted him. He managed to survive the indifference of the social workers who resented his bitter attitude. He managed to survive being in and out of jail for minor offenses because he happened to have a juvenile record. Jerry finally settled down, married, started to raise a family, opened an appliance repair shop. He had at this point a good family life and five happy children.

Then tragedy struck. Jerry's wife was killed in an automobile accident. Jerry tried to drown his sorrow in drink and that, he says, was when he met the girl, in a bar. Jerry's story was that she seemed older and that she agreed to go to bed with him, for a price. He said that the next morning she raised her price but that he refused to pay the extra amount and that she hollered for the police. Because of his prior record, Jerry is now serving a twenty-year sentence for rape. A lot of people will say Jerry got what he deserved but I don't believe it. Jerry needs help and understanding and friendship and to be given a chance to live down his past mistakes and live a good life tomorrow.

While seemingly responsible citizens continue to play their childhood game of cops and robbers, human lives are at stake and society is being paralyzed by a soaring crime rate. During the past twenty-five years, I have talked to convicted criminals in prison in California, Maine and Ohio. As a result of my examination of the unguarded workings of the criminal mind, I have obtained a deeper understanding of the people society labels criminal. Most convicts, I have found, just like the square johns they claim to hate and despise, are also playing a childish game of cops and robbers. Only they learned the rules of the game as they apply to the robbers. The professional criminal would rather die than betray the image of the "bad guy" that he has spent his life creating. No matter what the cost in destroyed lives and abused rights, he will cling to this distorted self-image to the bitter end. He will try to resist all efforts of society to rehabilitate him and alter his firmly rooted anti-social attitudes.

Surprisingly, many of the criminals I have met have been very moral people. But most of them have a blind spot. To the safecracker, his artful opening of a safe is a highly developed skill of which he is very proud. The burglar too justifies his nightly prowling as the work of a master craftsman. The check forger can see no connection between his clever fraud and crime in the streets. Regardless of intelligence, the professional criminal usually projects an inconsistent image of himself. Those distorted rationalizations are the hallmark of most criminals.

The non-professional criminal, most of our social failures that is, such as sex-offenders, alcoholics, drug addicts, all seem to have a built-in self-destructive urge that compels them to outrage fellow citizens. Perhaps, as some psychologists theorize, this type of offender is really only trying to get rid of deep feelings of guilt, probably harbored since early childhood. This aspect of criminal psychiatry needs a great deal more study before we will be able to deal effectively with the problems of our social failures.

We must first recognize that our prisons are little more than warehouses filled with the rejects of society. We are fooling ourselves if we pretend that prisons can effectively combat crime. Not all inmates of prisons are criminals. Many of them are people with crippling problems which they have not learned how to solve. Nor does it take a judge or a trained social worker to understand that criminals are just ordinary human beings with problems. The criminal is usually a person who has not learned to live and work with other people. He really needs help, not punishment.

On the Outside

XXXXXXXXXXXXXXXXXXXXXXXXXXXXXXXXXXXXXXXXXXXXXXXXXXXXX

"Want a transistor radio without paying for it? Its quite easy to steal any one you want. Want a brand new sweater or skirt? It won't cost you a dime. I can tell you how to get any article of clothing you want without paying.

"Shoplifting is the easy way to get what you want without paying! Shoplifting is getting to be really big business. Last year, for example, amateur and professional shoplifters got away with over eight billion dollars worth of merchandise without paying a single cent.

"Sound cool to you? Keep reading.

"Did you know that most shoplifters take things just for fun? But if you are going to shoplift, you might as well do it right. Here are some tips to make you the best shoplifter on your block.

"If you are a beginner, you might try switching the labels on merchandise in the store. You can switch the label from a cheap item to an expensive item. Won't it be fun to walk out of the store with the expensive item which you paid the cheap price for? If you want to really be daring, you can carry a large shopping bag and just go round the store dumping what you want into the open bag. Some professionals use a box with a false spring bottom. They just slip the box over the object they plan to steal. Its really quite a lot of fun. Most shoplifters don't even need the things they steal. If you are already bored with the amateur stuff, you might want to step into the big time and be like the professional boosters. You first must learn how to carry large, bulky items hung between your legs while you walk nonchalantly out of the store. A large topcoat often helps conceal the rip off.

"While shoplifters come in all ages and sizes, teenagers seem to be the largest number of practitioners in the field. Shoplifting is one of the largest and most pressing crime problems among teenagers in our country today. This is not just because of the merchandise which is lost but because it causes young people to think of crime as a game. It helps wear down the young person's feelings of honesty and morality.

"Lets look at Sammy Brooks, for instance. He is now serving a long prison sentence for grand larceny. But Sammy has never thought of himself as a thief. 'I only took the stuff for the fun of it,' he told the judge. But the judge wasn't laughing. Especially as Sammy had a record for shiplifting that went all the way back to the first grade. Sammy had started out innocently enough, just picking up things that he wanted without regard for the fact that they belonged to somebody else.

"A lot of smart kids who haven't been busted yet will tell you that guys who get caught like Sammy are dumb. They may be right. Every thief in prison today was at one time a smart kid, until he got caught.

"So let me wish you luck on your shoplifting career. The stuff you steal won't cost you a dime. But there may be just one small hitch. In one prison alone where I served time, the total time being served for theft amounted to over 30,000 years among all the convicts. If you insist on shoplifting after hearing all this, go ahead and get your kicks. Shoplifting won't cost you a dime. It *may* cost you a lifetime in prison."

A young girl from Fort Worth Texas read one of my weekly columns in the Fort-Worth Star-Telegram and wrote to tell me that she had just been caught stealing a balloon in a supermarket and that her parents had given her a sound spanking for it. Obviously, her parents cared enough about her to punish her swiftly and fairly. The experience, I hope, will keep her from experimenting again in this way for the rest of her life. If I thought my son believed in me as much as this girl believed in her parents I'd be quite happy.

Another girl wrote to tell me about a friend of hers

who was shoplifting for fun. She decided that the best way she could help her friend was to show her my article on shoplifting from which I have quoted at the beginning of this chapter. Apparently, it did some good.

You see, most kids who get into trouble in this way aren't really bad in the beginning. They are merely trying to find out how far they can go with their freedom. They want to see how far they can push their luck before the police or other authorities crack down on them. Unfortunately, some of them go too far and do end up serving a prison sentence. You can usually spot the young person who is heading for this kind of trouble. When a young person thinks that the laws only apply to other people, not to him or her, you have met a potentially dangerous rebel. He can lead you into serious trouble as well as ruining his own life. The problems of the shoplifter are not always easy to understand. In many cases the shoplifter is really a very lonely person who only wants to attract attention in this way. On the other hand, a friend's concern may help the young shoplifter to snap out of it.

More and more stores today are taking shoplifters into court. They are tired of sustaining such big losses year after year. As for the boys and girls who didn't really need what they were stealing, who thought they were playing a game, the store personnel seldom think of it that way when they call the police to have the shoplifters arrested, taken to court and punished.

I received a letter from a young lad in Cleveland. Here is what he had to say about stealing cars:

"Most old fogeys," he writes, "they don't understand us. They don't even try. They don't know how boring school gets day after day. Why should life be all work and study anyhow? Any hip kid can tell you that when you get bored one of the real highs in life is to steal a car and take your buddies joyriding. Man, its so easy to steal a car! People have too much money and they're so careless with their stuff, especially their cars. You can walk down the street and find plenty of cars with the keys still in the ignition— some assholes even leave their motors running for you. A kid would have to be a fool to let a chance like that go!

" Even if you get caught, its real easy to get away with it. All you have to do is act innocent and tell the owner you didn't mean any harm. Like if you tell him you only took the car to have some fun with your friends. You know, stand in front of where you put the dent in his fender so he won't see it; I mean, a thing like that might make him mad and he'd really press charges if he saw it. Act misunderstood. That always gets 'em. Most adults feel real guilty about kids, about not doing enough to help them. It really turns them on. Unless you get an old-fashioned jerk who still believes in law and order and all that. Then you'd better forget it. He'll file charges every time. But you won't find too many of them. Mostly you'll get off with just a warning. Most kids do. I know one dude who rips off a new set of wheels every week. He's got a line for conning the owners that's poetry in action. Man, you can get away with anything if you've the nerve to pull it off!

"If you're one of the lucky ones who don't have

NEWTON COUNTY LIBRARY

parents who try and lay a lot of bullshit on you about
law and order and right and wrong, you can really
have a blast. A lot of kids have parents who are still
living in the dark ages. Like they think their kids
should respect them and live the good life. One kid
I knew had parents that told him to respect the rights
of others. Man, what rights? Can you imagine a kid
like that ever getting it together to rip off a car?

"A group of kids here in Cleveland really got their
shit together. Like you can get traced through your
fingerprints and get caught, right? So they poured
gasoline all over the car and burned it after they got
through with it. The only problem these dudes had
is that they got caught doing it and then they got sent
to the reformatory for car theft and arson. I guess
they didn't think they'd get busted for two felonies
instead of one. Well, you can't win them all!"

As I read this hip kid's letter I realized that he
missed a lot of important points. My guess is that his
parents never punished him when he did wrong or
praised him when he did well. If you are one of those
kids who can do what you want without parental
control, you probably think you are really lucky. Well
let me tell you that most of the swingers I've met in
prison over the years were there because nobody
cared enough about them to help them see the differ-
ences between right and wrong when they were
kids.

I remember a rather frightening conversation I
once had in prison with a young man who was serving a sentence for armed robbery. This twenty-eight

year old was first arrested at the age of eighteen for auto theft and had been in jails almost continuously for ten years. What shocked me most was his almost complete lack of any feeling of guilt or responsibility for his actions. He felt only that he had been unduly and severely punished for his original offense of stealing a car. "After all," he reasoned, illogically, "I only had the car for five hours." It never occurred to him that taking the car in the first place might have been wrong. He believed that it was his right to "borrow" any car that appealed to him. Nor was he concerned for the rights of the man who owned the car.

That first crime had just been the beginning for this confused lad. "I met a real cool guy," he told me, "an older guy about thirty-five. He always made me feel important. He showed me how easy it was to rob a supermarket and get loads of money so that we could travel all over. He had the gun and I just went along to scoop up the money. We got away all right for a while but then we got caught. He's free right now while I'm still serving time. I learned from older crooks how easy it is to stick up places. I escaped from prison once. That's when I became a holdup man. I got me a gun and started out holding up places. It was real easy. I never thought about what would happen if I had to shoot somebody. I guess I would just have shot them. I'd have had to protect myself, wouldn't I?

"Whenever I needed money I could always go out and pull off a job. The guy who taught me, he never had any money left after he pulled off a job. He spent it all on booze and women as fast as it came in. And then he'd have to go right out and rob another store. Hell, there was no end to it. We were bound to get caught."

This convict had not yet killed anyone. The next time might be different.

Joe Roberts was already becoming a hold-up man in the fifth grade. He started by stealing money from his brothers and sisters. When he was caught he would get mad and dare his brothers and sisters to do something about it. This always worked. Nobody wanted any trouble. Joe's parents couldn't control him. Joe became bolder. He stole lunch money and other things from other children at school simply by demanding that they hand over to him everything that he wanted. While he was still in grade school, he threatened another child with a pocket knife. The victim was scared to report Joe's theft of his lunch money to the principal because Joe had threatened to "get him" if he did. As a result, Joe learned that he could terrorize the other children. He got away with this behavior for over a year before he was caught.

As a fourteen year old reformatory inmate, Joe met older, more experienced young criminals, who taught him a great deal. When he returned home from the reformatory, he found that he had dropped far behind in school. The children his own age now made fun of Joe. He really wanted to go back to school and get an education so that he could some day get a good job and be like everyone else. But it didn't work out that way for him. He was a far more successful thief than student.

Joe Roberts bought a gun. He robbed stores and then banks. One day when he tried to get away after a bank robbery, his car wouldn't start. Trying to flee on foot, he was caught by the police. He spent his time in prison daydreaming about future robberies he would commit as soon as his prison sentence was completed. Joe finally left prison a grown man with less than an eighth-grade education. What hope can there be for Joe Roberts and the millions in prison just like him?

Putting a burglar in prison seems to do little good. As soon as he gets out, he will probably go right back to his dangerous profession. It is usually the only job he knows.

Burglars and hold-up men fall into two categories: amateurs and professionals. The professional thief will have nothing to do with the amateur robber, who, on the street as in prison, is a lonely, frightened and inadequate person.

The greatest number of armed robberies and street hold-ups committed each year are the spur-of-the-moment acts of nervous and impulsive amateurs. The amateur robber is frequently a junkie, desperate for money with which to buy narcotics. He may be a thrill-seeking neighborhood kid anxious to increase his status with the gang he hangs out with or perhaps he is after some bizarre kind of sexual gratification. This type of criminal doesn't know from one moment to the next what he will actually do. No planning goes into his crime. He is not capable of assessing its outcome. If he happens to have possession of a weapon, he may shoot or stab his victim if the demand for money or dope is not met. He may kill to avoid detection or commit a senseless murder out of panic.

The public should realize the danger inherent in

this kind of a situation and act accordingly. It does absolutely no good to play the role of hero with the armed robber. Don't try to outsmart him as your life may depend on doing exactly what he tells you. You must remain calm and make a mental note of everything you see and hear. If and when the robber is caught, you will be more valuable as a live witness than as a dead hero. Every stick-up man is a potential killer; don't forget this.

One hold-up man in California claimed to have been earning a steady income of over 27,000 dollars a year. The frightening thing about this armed robber is that during the excitement of the robbery he would black out. He cannot recall a single incident of any hold-up he has committed.

The professional burglar, on the other hand, is in your home, store, bank or factory for one thing only. He wants money or valuables that can quickly and easily be turned into cash through his fence. The professional would rather make his escape than harm or threaten to harm someone he encounters during a burglary. The professional robber is also a unique kind of criminal because he will seldom engage in any other kind of crime. He has deliberately chosen his illegal profession as his way of making a living. The professional burglar or "cat man" may spend most of his life learning how to get in and out of locked buildings. He gains his entrance by skill and stealth and knows which things of value to take. The customary pattern is for the young student burglar to learn his trade from an experienced older cat man.

One burglar I knew started his career at the age of twelve when he just happened to notice an open window in a neighbor's house. He knew the neighbor was out of town so he crawled in to look around. But after he got inside he decided to help himself to whatever he found of value. And that was when a professional burglar was born. There was, he found, a big market for the things he was stealing from homes and stores. At one time in his career, this burglar even had a shopping list from which he worked. He had customers who actually ordered particular goods which he was to steal (gave him orders, that is, which he went out to fill by theft).

No matter where you hide your valuables, the experienced burglar has an instinct for finding them. Jake Marr, a professional "cat man" who told me a lot of inside secrets of the trade, recently advised me that the best place to hide money or valuables is right out in the open. The burglar will be so busy looking for clever secret hiding places that he'll trip over your valuables without finding them. If you wake up some night and discover that your home is being burglarized remember that noise and light are the principal enemies of the burglar. However, don't turn on all the lights at once. The burglar may be a keyed-up amateur or a junkie who will kill in order to escape, so do not try to corner him. Instead, lock your bedroom door, turn on the lights and make a lot of noise. If neighbors are close by, shout out for help and phone the police yourself if you have a telephone in your bedroom. According to Jake, the best protection against burglary is to buy a lot of insurance!

The "cat man" may work alone or with others. He may be part of a team composed of safecrackers and other professional thieves. A safecracker is called a "pete man" in underworld slang. The really good safecracker is usually a top-flight professional. He knows all about safes and how to break into them. He also knows how not to break into them.

Harry Krueger is a highly skilled "pete man" who knows his trade thoroughly. Harry first goes to work when he "spots" a safe in some place of business which he judges likely to hold a large payroll or perhaps a lot of cash from some special sales event. The first and most important step is to get close enough to the safe to study its particular characteristics carefully. It is also at this point, the "casing" of the safe, that the "pete man" is most vulnerable to detection. The police departments of most cities keep books of mug shots of top professional safecrackers and it is by means of these special photographs that most "pete men" are identified later.

A safecracker is as different from the burglar as cat from dog. But few really skilled professional "pete men" remain in operation today. Most safe jobs now are carried out by amateurs who kidnap a safe, often beating it to death to no avail or blowing it up just to get it open. The professional safecracker has strong contempt for the amateur. As Harry Krueger told me with obvious disdain in his voice, "if you gave these fools a can of beans, they'd sit there and starve to death before they could get the can open." He told me of how he once bought a safe from a panicky bunch of amateurs who had kidnapped it and completely failed to get it open. He paid them a thousand dollars for the safe and after he had calmly and professionally worked it open, he found 28,000 dollars inside in easily negotiable small bills. Like all professional safecrackers, Harry takes pride in his work and regards every single safe as a special challenge. His object is to outsmart the safe manufacturer and to get the door open with a minimum of damage to the safe and its contents.

Harry has been a loner most of his life to avoid endangering other people's lives. "And besides," he adds with a grin, "you can't really depend on any kind of help you'd get today. I guess the best advice I could give to a would-be safecracker these days, would be to forget all about it and go out and get a regular job."

Most burglars are desperately in need of help to solve their problems. But they don't know how to seek that help. They don't know how to stop being criminals. And most citizens aren't really interested in helping criminals to salvage their lives so that they could perhaps become honest, taxpaying citizens. Most citizens are afraid of criminals and would prefer to keep them in prison, out of sight and out of mind.

A less easily recognizable type of thief is the professional confidence man. Take Tom Hoya for example, whose official prison records warns: "do not believe anything this man tells you. His personal history is highly contradictory."

When you first meet Tom, you see a guy with an easygoing, friendly manner that will put you immediately at your ease and completely take you in. He can convince you of the truth of the most fantastic stories. He will verbally disarm you with eloquent promises. He is an expert manipulator, knowing just how to distract you by answering your questions with questions of his own. Con man to the core, his sole purpose is profit for himself. Tom Hoya earned himself a ten-year stretch for trying to buy a multimillion dollar chain of hotels for a Panamanian Syndicate that existed only in his fertile imagination. Not only was there no syndicate, there was no money in the bank on which Tom drew his large expense checks. When he was caught, Tom had to surrender his racing cars, luxury apartments, his women and his box at the race tracks.

The professional con man's stock in trade is lies. And the tragedy is that he seldom realizes that he is lying not only to others, but, more importantly, to himself. Under the attractive man-of-the-world mask, most con men hide a lonely, grotesquely insecure person who desperately seeks to be all things to all men. The best way to protect yourself from criminals like Tom Hoya is by being honest yourself. Stop being greedy, don't try to get something for nothing and don't let yourself be rushed into quick decisions however good the proposition sounds. Also, if you've been taken in by a con man, never be ashamed to admit your gullibility, for the con man knows how to exploit the common weakness that will make you not want to appear foolish in front of others. This is the way he avoids arrest and conviction. At this moment, Tom Hoya is in prison dreaming up schemes to relieve you of your hard-earned cash. As soon as he finishes his sentence he will put his plans into action.

However, as Harry Krueger the safecracker says, a thief, by the nature of his life-style, never gets rich. Even though he, for instance, may have from time to time gotten a lot of money by cracking safes, its always "easy come, easy go." Saving appears to be impossible for this kind of thief. The real big money is made by the lawyers, the bondsmen and the fence. (The fence is usually a respectable businessman who disposes of "hot" merchandise for the burglar.) The crook takes all the risks and the lawyers and bondsmen get all the gravy. And when you quit paying for their services, it's the pen, for you. "I can get into any safe made by man," says Harry, "but I haven't learned how to keep from getting caught."

That's the lesson which most men in prison really want to learn.

To Punish or Correct

We love to read the details of criminal acts in our newspapers and to watch gangster movies and television crime series. Most of us seem to share a perverse curiosity about violence, murder and sadistic sexuality. Yet we quickly and righteously condemn and punish those people who commit such acts against our fragile social values. Are we really punishing the criminal or are we vicariously punishing ourselves because we are secretly terrified that our own emotional controls will fail us? When we punish an offender severely is it because he or she performed an act that we didn't dare to do ourselves?

87

Society refuses to think clearly and honestly about crime, its complex causes or the best ways to treat it. We have to face up to the truth that it is society which produces the criminal, that everyone is capable of committing criminal acts, and that the indifference of citizens who refuse to even think about the new information piling up about criminality and its causes, is a crime in itself.

Whatever the evidence to the contrary, the general public seems somehow to be convinced that prisons do attempt to rehabilitate their inmates. In actual practice, prisons do little more than punish. I am convinced that prisons as they are run today do far more harm than good. Most convicts leave prison in worse shape than when they went in. It is wishful thinking to believe that the system as it operates today can correct, retrain or reform criminals in any meaningful way. The F.B.I has indicated that there is a direct link between our prison system and the rising national crime rate. Our prisons are the real training grounds for the expert and violent criminals in our midst.

Most prison wardens and superintendants will tell you that their primary function is neither to correct nor rehabilitate but to punish the inmates. Their job is to keep large numbers of convicts penned up in cages until the parole board says some of them can go home again. Far from retraining convicts and helping them to gain insight into their lives so that they could stay out of prison in the future and lead useful lives, prisons for the most part brutalize their inmates. Convicts have to endure whatever indignity or brutality an underpaid prison guard heaps upon them and keep their mouths shut about it. Because they are considered to be the garbage of humanity they are thrown on the junk pile, out of sight and mind of the rest of humanity.

It seems to me that confining people in prisons is a terrible waste of human life. Just take a look at the damage imprisonment does to human beings. The total loss of personal freedom would make anybody hostile and suspicious. The condition which in prison jargon is known as "prison paranoia" teaches a human being to hate and distrust every other person even when there is no logical reason for doing so. Life without normal sexual outlets also increases the terrible frustrations. Jack London, author of *Sea Wolf,* among many other famous novels, expressed amazement at the ability of men cooped up in a ship (or prison), to perform fantastic acts of courage and at the same time explode in rage over petty minor irritations. Life in prison is made up of many such daily irritations. Emotional explosions are the general rule. It takes a courageous man indeed to survive such a life. Few of them make it.

The correctional system could be compared to a patient entering hospital for an appendectomy and coming out with a terminal case of cancer. This analogy might seem odd. After all, people are not put in prison because they are sick. But as I hope I have shown, crime may be caused by physical or psychological disabilities. Many men and women in prison today are the victims of social circumstances from which they cannot extricate themselves. A person might have turned to crime as a desperate final effort at survival. Perhaps he cannot earn enough money to

buy food for the family, perhaps he is unskilled and
can never break away from the poverty cycle. Some
criminals are the victims of compulsive behavioral
patterns related to alcohol, drugs, sex and other
problems.

Many convicts are aware that they are behind bars
because they did not have enough money to pay for
a proper legal defense. They could not afford the
high-priced services of attorneys who might have got
them off. This is unfortunately a very important factor in the present criminal justice system of the
U.S.A. Money does talk. The system works against
the poor citizen, the ignorant, the minority groups,
the social failures who feel like pawns in a gigantic
game of chess. The wealthy person who is convicted
of a crime is usually given the chance to make a deal
with the county prosecutor to earn probation by paying a large fine, equal to or larger than the amount
the county would have received from the state for his
upkeep in prison. In this way he also avoids a permanent prison record. Convicts are bitter because of
this inequity. They are also bitter because they know
that 80 to 90 per cent of all criminals go unpunished
and that in one area of the country, the same offense
will get a longer sentence than in another area. They
soon come to suspect that they are not being punished for breaking the law as much as for being failures at crime.

Suppose you had known only failure all your life?
Do you think you would have any expectations of
future success? Quite frankly, I do not think that any
human being is too far gone to benefit from friendship. But it takes people with courage to involve

themselves with helping social outcasts to make successes of their lives. It takes time and effort to show these people that they can "belong" in the community. The alternative is to throw them on the waste piles of society—the prisons. Prison harshly punishes the convict for past failures while giving him no encouragement for good behavior. Real rehabilitation would have to expose the convict to values other than those which got him into trouble in the first place. Prisons today generally do not offer him alternatives to his former life style; instead they tend to reinforce all the negative things he knows and feels about an exploitative society and to increase his bitterness. I have seldom met a convict who was totally unsalvageable, but the prisons are doing their best to waste human lives and resources. Three and a half million lives seems a very big price to pay for our indifference.

It seems to me that we cannot place a dollar value on a restored human life. Yet, the loss in resources and human potential which is the product of our prisons might also be evaluated by the millions of state dollars spent on perpetuating the system. Some day the man in the street must get tired of supporting these wasteful and ineffective programs—prisons, reformatories and training schools which do not rehabilitate, or train, or in any way help the offender. It costs the taxpayer up to six thousand dollars each year to keep one convict locked up uselessly in prison. On the other hand, it would only cost about three hundred dollars a year to keep the same man in the community, under close supervision, on parole or probation, where he will pay his own way, earn a

salary, keep his family off welfare and live a law-
abiding life. Both society and the offender would
benefit from this approach but so many people are
unwilling to examine the facts and figures objec-
tively. They continue to pour millions of dollars of tax
money into an archaic prison system which does not
correct, does not reform, simply does not, in any
sense, work. If legislators cannot be convinced of the
potential dollar savings of correction versus punishment, it will become the job of the younger generation to bring these facts home.

According to an article in *Look* Magazine, the
State of California has saved eighty-one million dollars a year and reduced its prison population to the
point where it may soon be possible to close its biggest prison, the archaic San Quentin. This was the
result of putting more people on probation. Prior to
this, California had a provision for payment to the
counties for convictions. Now the State of California
pays the separate counties for every offender put on
probation.

The State of Ohio, for example, pays a bounty to
each county for every person who is sentenced to
prison. That is, when a citizen of Ohio is convicted of
a crime and sent to prison, the county is sent a check
to repay them for the expenses of the trial, extradi-
tion, and detainment of the prisoner. If, on the other
hand, the convict is given probation, the county loses
whatever it has spent on him up to this point. It
should be obvious that this kind of bounty system
increases the number of convictions. No matter how
fair the judge might be, he is a political person dependent on the votes of the citizens to retain his job

and subject to pressure from the county commissioners and the public to sentence more and more offenders to prison.

Ohio recently embarked on a plan which is proving effective: the State Legislature enacted a "shock probation" law which allows the county to sentence the offender to prison; collect the bounty from the state; and then release the felon after thirty, sixty, ninety days of the sentence. The theory is that a first-time offender will be given just enough of the taste of prison life to deter him from a life of crime. As far as I have been able to discover, the plan is working well with fewer than ten per cent of the offenders being given shock probation returning to prison. However, the offender is still a loser since he now has a prison record which he will never be able to live down.

Professionals in the area of criminal justice have long been aware that punishment alone is not and never has been an effective deterrent to crime. It does not, even in the case of the ultimate punishment, death, serve as a deterrent to others. Sociologists love to tell the story of pickpockets roaming through the crowds during a public hanging in old England, merrily robbing the pockets of those who watched the execution of another pickpocket!

The death penalty in recent years was in most cases exacted only for first degree murder in the U.S. That is, it was necessary to prove that the accused did willfully and knowingly plot to take another person's life. Murder and how we punish those who commit it is one of the most misunderstood aspects of our criminal justice system. Although there seems to be some public sentiment for bringing back the death penalty, there is no evidence to prove that states which did not exact the death penalty had a higher incidence of willful homicide than those which did.

Over the centuries, various means have been used to execute convicted murderers and other criminals. In France, the method used was the guillotine, a sharp weighted blade which severed the head from the body. Such executions took place as public entertainment, amid a carnival-like atmosphere. These spectacles, needless to say, did little to deter crime and provided the occasion for other criminal acts to take place. In England, convicted criminals used to be hung. In the U.S., death by firing squad in some states was replaced by the gas chamber and the electric chair which apparently was considered to be the most humane method of execution. It hardly requires pointing out that nobody who was executed has ever returned to complain or testify.

When the U.S. Supreme Court struck down the death penalty as administered in most state courts, it was not the humaneness of the penalty which was at issue but rather that "as presently administered" it was unfairly and unjustly discriminatory and therefore unconstitutional. The theory was that the death penalty would be fair and equal only if everyone who committed first-degree murder was executed. However, as the system worked, a black or poor white was far more likely to be executed than a wealthy white.

It must also be understood that first degree murder is very difficult to prove in a court of law. A great many persons originally accused of first-degree murder are eventually convicted of second-degree mur-

"... the seeds of crime bear bitter fruit"

der which means that pre-meditation is absent. The penalty for second-degree murder varies from twenty years to life imprisonment. One of the principal objections to the use of capital punishment is the possibility of error. I have been in prison with several men convicted of first-degree murder who were subsequently proved to be innocent of the crime when the real murderer confessed. I have seen this often enough in my lifetime to give me serious doubts as to the fairness and impartiality of our judicial system.

One of the biggest problems that prevents objectivity in dealing with the crime of murder is the terror that the act inspires. Statistically, however, most murders are not committed in cold blood, but are the result of sudden, uncontrollable emotion. They are largely unplanned and the victim is typically a member of the murderer's immediate family or a very close friend or lover. Anger is a powerful emotion and the act is most often committed in the course of a violent argument. At this point, when a person has lost control of his emotions, many of us would be capable of murder. Once the fit of violent emotion has passed, it is often too late and the murderer will spend a lifetime of remorse. Once in prison, such murderers are usually the most tractable, best behaved and least dangerous inmates there. Few of them would ever commit a second violent crime.

The most terrifying kind of murder is the kind committed during the course of a robbery. Another kind is when a kidnapper kills his victim to avoid detection. These kinds of murderers will get a very long prison sentence without the possibility of parole in most cases. A kind of murder which is becoming more and more common and disturbing is legally called manslaughter and may result from drunken or negligent driving.

During my imprisonment I have also met teenagers who are in prison for killing friends or their parents. Many of these killings could have been avoided if trained social workers or other interested adults had noticed the deep and apparently uncontrollable rage and hostility of the young person. When such a murder takes place it not only ruins the life of the murderer but damages the family of the murderer and that of the victim as well.

Such psychological and social problems desperately need help. Inside prison, there are not always educated and competent professionals available to help the prisoners. Some prisons still have no trained professional psychiatrists or social workers. Because of very low starting wages, most prisons depend on recent college graduates with little or no actual prison experience, but this is certainly better than having absolutely no trained psychologists or psychiatrists available to the convicts. More professionals are now being educated to work in this important area. Psychiatric and social workers must not only be highly trained, they must have genuine compassion and dedicated interest in the special problems of convicts. There are at this time not nearly enough of such people to make an impression on rehabilitation programs where they do exist. Let us hope that state legislators will see the need and vote the money to hire the professionals needed to help the prison inmates soon.

Many rehabilitation programs are hopelessly inadequate. One prison out west believes that two baseball diamonds paid for entirely out of inmate commissary funds is rehabilitation. Another prison which makes pottery to sell for the state's general fund considers pottery-making rehabilitation. One state believes that keeping the "lousy creeps" locked up day and night in crowded cells will make the convicts repent and that is their idea of rehabilitation. Nobody in the correctional field today agrees about what effective correction or rehabilitation consists of.

The closest I myself ever came to a sound rehabilitation program was at Chillicothe Correctional Institute where I had been confined. Here, the guards and civilian staff treated the inmates like human beings. It was the kindness and interest of a man called Bill Whealon which led me to my rehabilitation. Convicts, like everyone else need someone in whom they can put their trust and who will not let them down. It seems to me that a meaningful type of contact with one other human being might be at the core of true correction and rehabilitation. In my own case, I found that as I developed meaningful relationships with the civilian and guard staff of the prison, I began to act in a more responsible way. The prison code of "going it alone" no longer filled my need.

It should be the job of all of us to reach the public offender and offer him a chance to belong to the society which he now victimizes. A person who has made it after leaving prison has a strong feeling of warmth and gratitude towards those who helped along the way. He also wants to prove to them as well as to himself that he can make it in a hostile world. It is difficult to teach a convict to trust other human beings and to become people-oriented. A key ingredient of personal reform is the realization on the part of the offender that it is entirely up to him whether or not he continues to lead a law-abiding life. He must not blame other people for his failures as he so often did in the past. He should learn not to live impulsively from day to day for his own limited short-

Mr. Torok is not too optimistic about the rehabilitation potential of many of today's prison systems. At Chillicothe, he noticed a marked difference. "Here the guards and civilian staff treated the inmates like human beings. ... as I developed meaningful relationships with them I began to act in a more responsible way."

range goals and appetites. He should be helped to develop a goal in life.

Part of the problem of the effective rehabilitation of the offender is his re-entry into the community. At the present time it is extremely difficult for men with prison records to get a job. Some prisons try to offer vocational programs to teach convicts a skill. But many of these programs are wasted. Can you imagine offering a retraining program to a middle-aged or illiterate man? Illiteracy is quite common in prison. While I was in prison at the Chillicothe Correctional Institute, I developed an interest in the problems of illiterate convicts and became involved in a tutoring program to help convicts teach other inmates to read and write. This was a most satisfying experience.

When it has proved possible to give convicts vocational job training, they will usually abandon their criminal behavior. The man in prison must be taught social skills so that he can survive in the complex modern world. It really costs us more in dollars and wasted manpower if we do not give convicts proper job training. Getting rid of the deep-rooted prejudices that prevent ex-convicts from getting good jobs should be everyone's task. Convicts can be restored to meaningful lives when other people are willing to become involved and keep them from being a permanent public burden.

Citizens' committees are being organized and given free access into prisons. This is the only hope for prison reform in the long run. Until the press and the public have complete free access to prisons, at all times, there will be continued abuses that the public will never know about. The press and the media

must bring these abuses to light whenever and wher-
ever possible. Real prison reform will not come about
until an enlightened and humane citizenry really
becomes involved.

Law and Order

Usually a criminal is arrested on the evidence of his finger prints and eyewitnesses. When he is first arrested, he is sent to the city or county jail where he is booked for his crime and frequently detained until the day of his formal trial. The trial is held to determine whether or not he is guilty of the crime for which he is accused. If he is found not guilty, he will be immediately set free. If the court finds him guilty, he will be sent to the state prison to begin serving whatever length of sentence the judge has determined.

What happens if a judge or jury makes a mistake

and sends an innocent man to jail? This does happen from time to time. Theoretically, the U.S. Constitution provides protection for all citizens to whom this might happen even as a routine mistake. Even the lowest convict in prison has the right of appeal to a higher court. He can appeal his case all the way up to the U.S. Supreme Court if he so wishes. If a man has, for instance, been given a life sentence for murder and is not satisfied that he received a fair trial, he can ask the courts to take another look at the decision of the court which originally sentenced him. If he is still dissatisfied, he can keep appealing his case all the way up the ladder of the courts until he reaches the Supreme Court. If the Supreme Court rules in his favor, he will be set free. If the Supreme Court rules against him, his original sentence remains binding.

Thus the legal machinery of the entire United States Government can be put into gear to protect the rights of every citizen. This "due process of law" as it is called, is a system theoretically designed to protect us all. You may wonder if this system is the best possible arrangement for providing justice for everyone. A lot of people today are asking the same questions. There are many things wrong with our present system of "due process," but there is no doubt in my mind that it is theoretically the best system in the world. If legislators were only willing to make it work more effectively, "Equal justice under the law" could become more than just a slogan in America. (In the chapter, *The Search for Justice,* I am going to discuss just what is wrong with the law as it is practiced).

Some people think that the concept of law and

order infringes upon the concept of individual freedom. Others think that you cannot have one without the other. There are many people in our democracy searching for answers to problems such as this one. The "common good" should be good for all people equally, regardless of their political, religious, ethnic or economic condition.

Ever since man banded together in tribal groups, he has sought to regulate the behavior of the other members to provide a conformity and protection for everyone. Whereas the laws that everyone agreed to in principle caused no conflict, the fair enforcement of these laws for all members of the tribe was the cause of much hardship. Favoritism always seemed to arise. In medieval times it was only the free-man who was protected by the law. In England the Common law was for the common people while aristocrats were governed by an entirely different code.

Consider for a moment being a lawmaker in the Pilgrim days and sharing in the creation of the laws that governed America's first settlements. Wouldn't you have been proud to know that your idea of freedom would be influencing future generations? But you may not have realized that you were in fact tying the hands of your grandchildren. In far too many societies, the descendants of the pioneers are the inheritors of a hand-me-down legal system which may have become burdened over the years with piecemeal additions and subtractions, producing a body of law which is motheaten, hidebound and sadly lagging behind the real needs of the people. Many of us, unfortunately, have lost sight of the fact that the law, in order to be enforceable as well as respected, must relate to the needs of a changing society. We have to continually examine and review our laws. People living in a dynamic space age have the right to be governed by laws that reflect the age they live in, not by laws drafted to meet the cultural needs of a dead generation.

Until fairly recently, the world was dominated by a farming culture and outlook. Large families supported themselves through raising crops. With the Industrial Revolution, we moved into a time when the majority of people came to inhabit cities and towns. And yet most of the laws in the statute books were enacted to deal with the problems of an agricultural society. Reapportionment of state legislature on the basis of real population instead of geographical boundaries is seen as an important step in the process of reform that will bring the body of law into a modern context so that all citizens will be able to respect it and abide by its dictums. If you are aware of the generation gap between parents and children, just imagine, if you can, the gap that must exist between the applicability of laws that were drafted over a hundred years ago to protect primarily rural interests and the laws that are needed today to protect a society where narcotics, perversion and crime in the streets are daily facts of urban life.

Our definition of law should be a relative definition and one that is redefined as times change. Laws that are outdated bring only scorn and disrepute on the entire body of law. The law should be able to equitably reflect the needs and aspirations of a rapidly changing society. It is undoubtedly gratifying for a generation of people to earn their own freedoms and carve out their own laws. But succeeding generations should not have to carry the burden of legal practice that has become archaic and possibly unworkable. The challenge to the children of the pioneers is to construct their own freedoms from the building blocks left around so conveniently by their ancestors.

What is individual freedom after all? To my way of thinking, it is the ability to do whatever we want to most of the time without physical and moral restraint or intimidation as long as such activities do not infringe on the freedoms of another. Although some philosophers claim that man is a slave to his emotions and can never really be free, many prisoners in chains and dungeons have in fact achieved philosophical freedom. As St. Paul noted so well: "The truth can make you free."

The free man may have accepted his personal responsibility for upholding the laws, those with which he disagrees as well as those with which he agrees. He recognizes his ability to change the laws he dislikes through the proper channels. He feels that the spirit of the law should be based on justice, welfare and morality and he wants the benefits of freedom to be available to all those willing to share in the responsibility for upholding it.

An outlaw or renegade, on the other hand, would deny other citizens their individual freedom. In almost every society, the outlaw has been denied equal protection under the law. To conform to the laws of the group was to provide liberty, stability, and a form of security within that society. That is something that many convicts in prison today cannot understand. They do not share Lincoln's belief that the fruits of

The Southern Ohio Correctional Facility, Lucasville, Ohio.

liberty should belong to those who uphold it. Why, for example, is the man in prison denied his freedom of movement? Can it be because he has rejected the concept of the dignity of other citizens? Does he use the goods, property and persons of others to achieve his own self-centered goals? Does he in fact enslave others to his own needs? Does he deny to others that freedom which he wants so much for himself? If that is the case, he is chained in another prison of his own making, a larger prison of greed and selfishness.

Behind bars, in his prison cell, the convict knows what it is like to be without individual freedom. He is physically restrained in a prison cell and practically his every movement and thought is regulated and limited. Most of us will never know what it feels like to be that totally restricted. Some people in foreign countries where liberties are restricted may know how it feels. Can you imagine what complete lack of freedom can do to a human soul? Can you imagine how degrading and dehumanizing such imprisonment can ultimately become? Whether the convict deserves such treatment at the hands of society is another matter. The judge, jury, prosecutor, the entire criminal justice process may consider that this state of servitude will reform him, will do him good. But nothing is further from the truth. More likely, prison will sharpen his criminal skills while increasing his hatred and desire for revenge against a society that has locked him away.

The convict in prison today is often walking a dangerous tightrope. He is trying to live his life free of conflict just like his free-world counterpart outside the prison walls. On the one hand he may find it necessary to please the men with whom he must spend his endless days and nights; on the other, he must be on the alert to please the prison guards who have power over him and can make his prison life a living hell on earth.

Caught in the Act

In a city that enforces its laws fairly for everyone and has strong community support for ethical behavior on the part of public servants as well as ordinary citizens, the policeman could be a proud and respected symbol of shared authority. In a city that tolerates corruption, the policeman may be the most corrupt.

Everywhere in America today, our police forces seem embroiled in controversy over what their job really is. Sometimes, you can't tell the cops from the robbers. Some people say the police are corrupt and no better than the criminals they arrest. Others say

they are the protectors of society. Some even say that
the policeman of today should be an expert counselor
in human relations and a neighborhood coordinator
and keeper of the peace. Other people say he is just
a "pig" hired to keep the streets clean and cool for
the establishment.

What is the true face of the policeman in America
today? The typical policeman is called upon to play
a multitude of roles that may or may not have anything to do with his job. The role he plays in any
community will reflect the needs and aspirations of
the place where he lives and works. Most cops today,
however, strongly object to the baby sitting chores
they are called upon to perform while major crime
runs rampant. For instance, six cops can be called to
break up a family arguement while barely a block
away, a gang of thieves is hauling away a safe in a
dimly lit business district. The cops are beginning to
look for help in the community from family counsel-
ors, ministers, laymen, lawyers, to help solve the
time-consuming noncriminal police business. Bill
Jones, for example, always wanted to be a policeman,
but when the sergeant at the station house found out
that Bill could type, he made him a clerk-cop. Bill
spent most of his time with the department making
out forms and doing the work of a secretary. Smart
police departments are now beginning to turn this
massive load of detail work over to qualified police
aides and secretaries who can do the work of typing,
answering the phone, booking prisoners, making
fingerprints and other noncriminal work so that the
police officer can return to his job of apprehending

criminals and protecting the community from crime. A midwestern city even shuffled its policemen around and added another complete shift of extra night-patrolling officers without hiring a single new man. By concentrating police "visibility" in high crime areas the city has cut its crime rate by fifteen per cent, which is a good record in any city.

It is estimated that there are half a million cops in our country today, which works out to about one cop to every five hundred citizens. Police officers are neither saints nor sinners. They are human beings just like the rest of us, trying to do their job as best they can. After all, its really the citizen who is the cop's boss, and the typical cop will only do what his community will tolerate, not much more and certainly no less. If our cops are corrupt, it may be because we are corrupt. If our cops are pigs then perhaps it is because we are also pigs. And if we have cops who are fair and honest, we are probably fair and honest too.

A good cop trying to do his job fairly may get spat at by an angry demonstrator. Because he is a good cop he'll wipe away the spittle and continue in his duty. Police Officer Henry Carter was known as a fair cop. At 11:00 A. M. one day, answering an emergency call to a middle-class neighborhood, he drove up to the scene of the alleged complaint. A man with a sawn-off shotgun walked up to the car, levelled the gun at Officer Carter's head and blew the young cop's brains out.

In the 1960's over 550 policemen were murdered. In the 1970's it looks as if the figure may be doubled.

A brutal cop on duty during a demonstration, repeatedly beat a young girl over the head and caused her permanent brain damage. Examples of this kind can always be found in the daily newspapers.

In prison, there are policemen too. The policeman in prison is called a guard or, in more modern prisons, a correctional officer. For the convict, he has other names, such as "screw" "bull" "hack" and many others which are mostly uncomplimentary. The prison guard escorts the convicts to and from their work and activities within the prison. He must prevent the convicts from escaping and from harming each other. He must always be on the alert. Some guards walk up and down on the thick stone walls that cut most prisons off from the outside world. Many prisons instruct new guards that they should never turn their back on a convict for any reason, that never, for an instant, should they trust a convict. This presumably is to prevent the guards from being surprised and overpowered in an escape attempt. Working in a prison can be dangerous work especially if it is one of the old-fashioned kind that stresses punishment rather than rehabilitation.

Keeping the peace inside a prison is not all that unlike keeping the peace outside the walls. There is crime inside a prison just as there is crime on the streets. A convict may steal something from another convict. A fight between inmates may result in violence. Guards also have the authority and power to arrest a convict for major or minor infractions of the prison rules. When this happens, the inmate will probably be taken to the detention cell often referred to as the "hole," for punishment. This is like being put in a prison inside a prison. In many states,

"Today an attempt is being made in many prisons to replace the old-fashioned 'kangaroo court' inside prison with a sympathetic panel of social workers, correctional officers and ministers to help the frustrated convict to work out solutions to his personal problems."

the offending convict can be put on a diet of bread and water for as long as the prison court may order. When the convict is tried and convicted by such a "kangaroo court" inside the prison, he knows he will not get a fair hearing from prison officials. No wonder he quickly loses respect for all justice in prison.

How to punish the prison inmate is a serious problem. For most courts, just being in prison is normally punishment enough. Usually there is no real justification anyway for further harrasment or punishment for minor rule infractions. Modern prison administrators are learning that it is better to substitute human concern for indiscriminate punishment.

The convict may feel lonely, abandoned, and frustrated because he is isolated in his small prison cell, cut off from normal human contact. He may lash out at the nearest prison guard as a way of expressing his hostility. This is an unfortunate byproduct of our repressive prison system. Warden Clinton T. Duffy, who was warden at San Quentin prison when I served my first sentence there twenty-five years ago, pioneered many reforms. He believed in treating convicts like human beings and many men were able to leave prison and live a good life because of the kindness of this pioneer penologist. However, many convicts in repressive prisons have been beaten and killed by brutal prison guards who did not share Warden Duffy's humane ideas.

Today an attempt is being made in many prisons to replace the old-fashioned "kangaroo court" inside prison with a sympathetic panel of social workers, correctional officers and ministers to help the frustrated convict to work out solutions to his personal problems. A convict who is able to respect law and order inside prison is more likely to become law-abiding when he is eventually released. Many prison guards are beginning to realize that, since they spend more time with the convicts than other people, they are potentially the best people to help the convicts to understand their problems and learn to correct their mistakes. This new breed of correctional officer learns to trust the convict until the individual shows by his own actions that he does not deserve that trust. Most inmates who are mean and violent have become that way because of brutal treatment by guards in prison. Many prison guards are trying to reverse that trend but there are still far too many prisons around in which convicts are still treated like animals in a zoo. When guards are not properly trained and not adequately paid to deal with human beings they become incapable of burying their own aggressions and hostilities when dealing with angry men. The convict in prison may resent being punished year after year for a crime he committed long ago with no chance to redeem himself in the eyes of society. The modern correctional officer can help this convict to change his attitude toward society and toward himself and to rebuild his life outside in the free world.

The Search for Justice

~~~~~~

What are the real causes of crime? The simple fact is that we do not today know the answer. Citizens are challenging the very nature of what crime is. A definition of crime is very hard to come by. The newspapers publish editorials about police reform, court reform, prison reform and all kinds of reform except the kind of reform which might bring into focus the causes of alienation and hostility in an affluent society.

Honest citizens are searching for a clear understanding of the principles underlying justice which protect human rights. Equal justice under the law is a must in any society that hopes to have its laws respected by all of its people at all times. Clearly, we need constitutional reform that will guarantee every American, of whatever color or economic condition, a fair hearing when conflicts arise. Some people claim that there is a critical problem because certain minority groups are seeking special privileges under the law. In actual fact this is far from the truth. Many Americans today have a hard time obtaining justice in our courts of law because of their inability to hire competent attorneys or to afford excessively high bail bond.

When people feel that they do not belong to a society, they will victimize and exploit that society. Every American citizen should be able to understand where he stands legally as well as morally in relation to the community at large.

The machinery of justice is a complete mystery to most of us. Our courts are clogged, our jails are jammed with the suffering, the sick, the inadequate, the unfortunate, the poor and the occasional criminal. Our prisons have become little more than warehouses for social failures. The imprisoned feel trapped in a system of laws that function more like a vacuum cleaner than a sensitive or humane tool of justice. It seems to me that we are living in the space age yet being governed by an ox-cart judiciary. Clearly, we need a new and workable definition of crime for a changing, mobile, affluent society where it should be possible for people to live and work in peace with one another.

State Penal Codes in the fifty states are a hopeless mish-mash of contradictory ethical, political, economic, moral and expedient nonsense. It is possible to step across an imaginary line and perform an act which is illegal on one side of the line but not at all criminal on the other side of it. In one state, you can be arrested, convicted and imprisoned for doing something for which you would be allowed to go free in another state, which might entail merely crossing the street. No wonder so many citizens feel no qualms about crossing the boundaries of good taste and morality. Just do your thing where it is legal and ethics be hanged. If you are confused, it is not surprising. Americans all over the nation are confused.

If you are unfortunate enough, under these circumstances, to run foul of our fascinating criminal justice machinery and find yourself accused of breaking a law which you do not understand, of doing something, for instance, which you did not know was illegal, it will be difficult to prove it. You will find yourself in the hands of public officials who will satisfy themselves somehow as to the facts and will then set about the process of detaining and prosecuting you. Like Pontius Pilate, two thousand years ago, they may wipe their hands clean with complete and unthinking justification.

Law and order is big business today in the United States. Many people owe their comfortable lifestyles and their childrens' college education to a job in correctional or law enforcement programs. It cannot be denied that there are many fine policemen and correctional officers. But there are also those who simply put in their time by wielding the vacuum cleaner of our laws with great relish and sweeping the gutters clean of derelicts, whereupon they point out with pride that they are keeping the streets safe. Safe for whom? For the crooks who are burglarizing offices and homes two blocks away and whose chances of being caught, prosecuted and sentenced are so minimal that it is considered worth the risk? In some parts of our nation both crime and the pursuit of the criminal are regarded as a game of chance. Many law and order officials see the pursuit of criminals in the same light that a hunter regards his licensed hunting: great sport and seldom boring. The criminal, if he can afford to pay, seldom has to play the prison game. If he can't afford to pay, he may be faced with the alternative of paying with the years of his life.

Comfortably assured meanwhile that all the problems of crime in the streets are in the hands of capable elected officials and the police, the man in the street wraps himself in a cocoon of false security. What most citizens fail to realize is that our system of justice is outmoded and often unworkable and that if it can victimize the lowliest of us today it might be the turn of the mightiest of us tomorrow. It is difficult for the man in the street to admit that he has given the officials he so blindly trusts nearly unlimited license, ostensibly to sweep our streets free of crime, while ignoring the cancer-like problems of organized crime and corruption that can be found throughout our society. The truth is that prisons are packed not so much with the kind of criminal one would expect as with the indiscriminate sweepings of society's gutters, that is, the failures at crime and the social outcasts. The real criminal, the master craftsman of crime, not infrequently glides serenely and peacefully through the intricacies of our criminal justice system, conveniently blinding the goddess of Justice with a thousand dollar bill.

The general public may think that the lawbreakers are safely behind bars, but less than three percent of our working criminals ever end up in prison. Most of the miserable citizens in prison are disturbed, helpless and hopeless human beings who perhaps tried to solve their intolerable problems in ways that were not socially acceptable. They have been branded as criminal and locked away in places where the chances of obtaining any help for their problems are practically nil. Putting them into concrete boxes with bars across the front, feeding them on schedule, providing for only the most basic of needs in clockwork fashion merely re-enforces the dependency of such people and perpetuates their roles as social outcasts.

Nearly two thirds of all arrests in any city are for things like drunkeness, disorderly conduct, vagrancy, gambling, prostitution and private sexual acts which are in reality nobody's business. These crimes may have outraged the sensibilities of others, they are probably violations of our moral code, but they do not actually require a victim. I do not personally believe that there can be such a thing as a "victimless crime;" altogether too often the real victim is the convict in prison who becomes the victim of the retribution inflicted upon him by an uncaring society. If we were to remove the so-called victimless crime from our criminal code, we would automatically and dramatically reduce the amount of crime that must be prosecuted. The police would then be able to concentrate their efforts on apprehending the real criminals.

"That's what they do to you, they turn you into a number."
(Quote from a prisoner at Ossining Correctional Facilities, in
Sing-Sing: The View From Within. New York: Winter House
Ltd., 1972.)

A book which very much influenced my thinking
on this subject, "Les Miserables" by Victor Hugo,
made Frenchmen and thinking people all over the
world wonder if their definition of crime was a realistic one. The book tells the story of Jean Valjean, a
poor man who was forced to steal to feed his starving
family during the French Revolution. For his single

crime he is pursued relentlessly by Inspector Jauvert, symbol of law and order, so that "justice" might be done. We are still struggling to define the concepts of justice and law and order. I shudder to think of a possible time when we will have reduced our search for justice to a set of rules and regulations to be parroted by mindless citizens.

In its simplest sense, the law should protect the innocent and should punish the guilty. The more humane a society becomes, the more will it try also to protect the guilty for whose behavior extenuating circumstances can be proved. For example, if a lawbreaker is truly insane, it would accomplish little to punish this person as would be the case with a sane criminal. Our democratic political system allows us to redefine what are criminal and what are anti-social acts. We must study the problems of changing social conditions and make changes in the law accordingly. We must overhaul the machinery of our ineffective judicial and correctional systems and then update the laws of all the states of the union to provide uniform justice based on realistic concepts of human and civil rights, morality and acceptable social norms.

In the area of punishment under the law, I do not believe that any prison today can correct any inmate. A prison might provide the tools with which a prisoner can bring about his own rehabilitation, but that is all. In my own case, my rehabilitation began when I was willing to accept the responsibility for my own actions as they affected others. But I was lucky in meeting good-hearted civilian workers in prison who helped me to understand myself, my motives and

reasons for my conflicts with the law. Not many convicts are so fortunate. Sad to say, most convicts find
that the values and ideals expressed by good people
are seldom matched by their actions. It has been my
good fortune, however, to witness what could only be
described as miracles performed by a group in Ohio
known as "Man to Man Associates." This group of
volunteers has agreed to match one civilian sponsor
with one convict in prison. The sponsor visits his
convict at least twice a month and writes him at least
once a month. Usually these convicts have not received visits or mail for a long time. They are the
forgotten men of our society. However, as a result of
this relationship, many of these convicts have decided to reform and stay out of prison.

It is ironic that most people think of justice only in
terms of the law, of police, courts and prisons. Perhaps more thought should be given to considering
the positive sides of this concept. I would like to
envision a time when human beings will become
more concerned for each other, more aware of the
responsibilities invovled in sharing this planet with
its growing numbers of people.

Meanwhile, many segments of the population no
longer respect unequal and unenforceable laws.
Lawyers and judges themselves have begun to question our laws and their functions. We too must guard
against the tendency to give blind support to a system of laws and controls that fails miserably to come
to terms with the changing human condition.

The Search for Yourself

XXXXXXXXXXXXXXXXXXXXXXXXXXXXXXXXXXXXXXXXXXXXXXXXXXX

I have found that most young people have uncommonly good judgment and common sense. Anxious parents to the contrary, I do not believe that the youth of today are political rebels. Long hair and exotic clothing do not turn good-hearted kids into dangerous revolutionaries or anti-social characters. Some adults are so disturbed by the few rebels and nonconformists they see storming across their television sets that they fail to realize that many of those characters are troublemaking attention-getters. Consequently they are unable to see that the vast majority of young people today are in reality idealists, law-abiding, respectful, individuals who are very concerned about their country's well-being. They are really no different from the young people of colonial days except that more goods and services are available to them.

Each new generation of teenagers believes that their generation is the first in the world to see public disturbances, riots and demonstrations against unchanging social problems. Apparently, a lot of kids forget what they read in their history books about the Boston Tea Party! As for student unrest and student riots, did you know that in Spain hundreds of years ago, university students actually tore an entire college campus apart brick by brick?

Most riots and demonstrations are the result of legitimate complaints by frustrated citizens against conditions which have become intolerable and which have not been corrected through normal procedures. Such demonstrations could be circumvented if concerned leaders were sensitive to the beginning sounds of discontent and dissatisfaction. When any governing body, whether of a school or of a country, becomes too big to listen to the smallest voice among us there will be disturbances and trouble. The wise people in authority who know this listen carefully and act when necessary. Kids today want to be involved in something worthwhile. If they can't find a cause that appeals to them, they will usually invent one. All things considered, I feel confident in the ability of today's youth to come to grips with the challenges of the future.

A real lack of effective communication between young people and their parents and other adults is at

the root of the difficulties affecting young people today. Parents do not seem to trust teenagers and teenagers no longer respect the views of older people. It
is not unusual for parents to violate the privacy of
their children by listening in to phone conversations,
opening personal mail, going through pockets and
even searching confidential diaries for clues about
what they are convinced is the child's path to de-
struction. How much more sensible it would be to
face one's children openly. As a matter of fact, most
young people prefer that their parents or guardians
exercise proper control over them with loving but
firm discipline. A loving parent can always punish a
child if it is done fairly. Usually, when a mutual trust
develops along with deep affection, the need for punishment disappears. A child from a secure, happy
home will seldom end up in prison.

How often have you heard your friends say that
they hate school and that school is just a waste of
time? You might be surprised to learn that many
convicts never got past the fifth grade. The problems
that cause a student to drop out of high school begin
early, usually when the child first enters grade
school. These problems are aggravated over the
years by inattentive parents, indifferent teachers and
uncaring adults. High school dropouts can come
from good homes in upper class neighborhoods just
as well as from low-income ghettos. Low I.Q. is not
necessarily a major feature of the drop-out picture.
Some drop-outs are merely bored with a school system which does not challenge them. A lot of them
have quit school to get a job which can support their
car. Too many schools in the past stressed academic

subjects to prepare the bright students for college. Educators are learning that this approach is not realistic. Most students need a basic education tied in with vocational programs to help them acquire a useful job skill. Many educators are now willing to work with each student to find the right program for his needs.

Job competition is getting tougher each day. The kid without a high school diploma has many options closed off. Each kid leaving school will need every advantage that he can muster. The young person who finishes school will earn from thirty to one hundred percent more in wages than the job seeker who is without a high school diploma. If you are thinking of dropping out of high school, try talking to your guidance counselor about it. If you can't talk to your counselor, seek out another interested adult with whom you can talk comfortably and freely, and who can help you to sort out your thoughts and feelings. Don't accept failure before you even start out in life. Too many people in prison quit school too early. Look where it got them! Drop-outs may seem to have all the fun, but they pay dearly for it in the end.

Most of the young people I know are searching desperately to learn who and what they are. They need all the help from adults they can get. Unfortunately, all too often adults are not aware of this need and do not listen attentively enough. There is a real challenge for adults to understand the real message in the words and acts of their children. Parents are often guilty of giving contradictory messages. For instance, I have heard parents telling their children that they wanted them to grow up to be strong individuals; and yet, when the son or daughter begins to express his or her individuality with long hair or stylish clothing, these same parents become hysterical with anger.

Young people are full of fears about themselves, about the changes that are taking place within their own bodies, in their personal world of feelings, their lives at home, at school and ultimately in the world. Are they or are they not homosexual; are they or are they not pregnant; should they date this or that person? How should they combat the deep and gnawing loneliness that is tearing them to shreds; should they run away from home or stick it out one more day?

Drug problems and alcohol problems emerge as primary problems bothering young people. Where can they find a sympathetic adult to listen to them? Will the hysterical parent calm down long enough to help find a solution? The young person wants to belong to his group at school or in his neighborhood but the pressures for performance within any group may be destructive beyond anything which previous generations have experienced.

When I was a kid, we didn't have drugs to experiment with. I guess beer and cigarettes were our ways of expressing our new-found and perilous independence. It wasn't difficult to persuade a grown-up to buy beer for my gang. We'd get a group together and scrape up enough cash for a party. Then, with cigarette smoke so thick it could be cut with a knife, we felt we were really in the big time. Surely we were not the first to discover alcohol and its euphoric benefits. Indian beer for instance was made, long before the Pilgrims arrived, out of fermented birch and maple sap. A lot of well-meaning people try to make a big thing out of modern kids drinking beer. I cannot see anything wrong with allowing young people to drink beer if they can handle it in a responsible way. Children in many countries of the world are raised on a diet of moderate amounts of beer and wine which they learn early to enjoy and respect. Tolerant and informed parents should actually be pleased if their children prefer moderate beer drinking to drugs.

Of course, whether adults like it or not, drug use has become a style of life for millions of young people. The difficulty is in determining which drugs may be used safely without running foul of the law and doing damage to one's health. Principal among the conflicts which young people have told me about in their letters, is the duplicity of their parents' attitudes when they tell them that drugs can harm their lives. Meanwhile these same parents are drinking, smoking and using all sorts of pills to "pick them up," "bring them down" or "help them over a rough time." Sleep problems, upset stomach, headache or discomfort anywhere in the body or mind call for yet another kind of chemical formula. The confusion young people feel when watching this escapist spectacle in their own homes and as advertised on television is especially keen when they are warned not to use a relatively harmless weed called marijuana. The fact that marijuana is against the law hardly seems worth mentioning when most young people realize that many of the drugs and nostrums used by their parents are far more harmful in the long run.

I am not and never have been a drug user. My interest in drugs and my ideas about their use are based on my daily contact with drug users and pushers in prisons for the past twenty-five years. I have known men and women who have been addicted to hard drugs for long periods of their lives and who were nearly always miserable despite the supposedly euphoric results of their habit.

A serious problem in modern life is boredom. This is a strong indictment of our society and a sign that we are in desperate need of new objectives, moral, spiritual, philosophical and intellectual. I have noticed that people who lack long-range or even short-range goals, drift in a state of depressed boredom from one experience to the next. The person who is alone and adrift in society, whether a member of a family or not, feels piercing anxiety and soul-tearing isolation. It is this isolation from the group, this loneliness, which causes most young people to turn to drugs. It has been found that drugs act in large measure as a substitute for the love and attention which all people crave and many lack.

In Chicago recently, a 22 year old prisoner named Timothy W. Chalfin just sat in his cell crying. According to the sheriff of McHenry County, Illinois, the man had only the night before tried to hang himself. He tore up a sweatshirt and then wrapped it around his neck. Tying the other end to the bars of the cell, he jumped. Another prisoner noticed the hanging man and called the sheriff who untied the young man and lowered him to safety in time. Tim Chalfin was apparently as unsuccessful in suicide as he was in everything else. Now he just sits in his jail cell, help-less, hopeless and in tears. Perhaps he is lucky. He is still alive.

Chalfin, who was in jail awaiting trial on an armed robbery charge, had expected to die. He left the fol-lowing note:

"Please tell my mom and dad I love them dearly and they have done all they could. If only the kids nowadays knew what they were doing to themselves when they take drugs. I pray to God someday they will. I want the money I will get back from the in-come tax to be used to pay back the man I took it from. Then I wish the rest to go to the police depart-ment to be put to use somewhere in trying to stop the drug abuse in this country. God please forgive me for my past. It's no one's fault but my own. I can't go on like this anymore. My flashbacks (hallucinations) have been getting worse. I didn't want to bother you about them because you have more important things. God have mercy on my soul."

It has been my experience that telling young peo-ple about the dangers of drug abuse will not keep them from experimenting. Most drug users are lon-ers. Perhaps that is why they are not interested in listening to the people who have gone the same road, to those currently in prison for drug offenses or who have died as a result of abusing their bodies through the heavy use of drugs.

Most of the addicts I have met and known in prison have been desperately lonely and embittered people who rejected everyone who tried to help or ap-proach them in any way. They have become bent on isolation and self-destruction. Suicide is often the

only workable solution in their eyes. I honestly believe that the use of drugs is a coward's alternative to
suicide. The single outstanding quality of the drug
addicts I have met, is their inability to face life as it
really is. Had they the courage, the chances are they
would have committed suicide. Like the alcoholic,
the typical drug addict turns away from other people
towards chemical and artificial remedies for his problems. And when the temporary remedy wears off,
the problems are still there. Why should I tell you all
the ways in which dope can ruin your health? You
probably know far better than I do. The thrill-seeking young person who plays games with death is a
close cousin to the grass smoker who defies the law.
Whether we like it or not, whether it is reasonable or
not, the use of marijuana is against the law. Just because everyone else seems to be breaking the law,
there is no reason why you should do so too. But if
you don't mind going to jail, go ahead and ignore the
law. As for trying hard drugs to see what they are
like, you might just as well jump from a twenty-floor
building to see if you will be hurt by the fall. You will
probably find that the free sample you are offered is
a trap. Once you start you will not be able to stop.
When your friends urge you to share a trip with
them, they might as well be sticking a knife in your
back.

Many innocent young children are started on the
road of drug use by well-meaning parents who want
to help their child over a sickness. Stronger and
stronger doses of a mild medicine become necessary
to feel relief. Even vitamin pills taken in excess can
encourage the tendency to drug dependency. Fur-

thermore, the taking of medicines and remedies for sickness may be simply covering up the real problems.

Children having trouble with school work may discover that taking pills helps them escape their problems. Soon they find they need more and stronger drugs. This may lead to stealing from their parents and classmates to support their growing need. Some children will risk grave danger when they experiment for fun with drugs offered by some older student or friendly stranger. Others have tried strange and powerful drugs rather than risk offending a friend who has invited them. When they get really hooked, they find that they cannot get along without drugs. The poor youngster who tries to stop may find he feels terribly ill. By returning to the drug in ever increasing doses he may feel better, temporarily. Children as young as nine years old have been found to be hooked for life on strong drugs. Even babies have been born addicted when the mother was using drugs during pregnancy. Not all dope sellers or users are strange wild-looking people with long hair and dirty clothes. They can be among the neatest, cleanest and nicest-looking kids in your own school.

Information and education about drug abuse is very necessary if young people are going to be able to understand the problems and make up their own minds. When someone asks you to sniff glue or take strange pills and powders, or eat sugar that tastes odd, or stick a needle in your body without a doctor's orders, warn him that if he persists, you will turn him in to the school authorities.

During the time I was in prison and receiving

thousands of letters from teenagers, I received this letter which I would like to share with you. I will also share my reply.

"Dear Mr. Torok:
When you said what you did about drugs in your Teen-Ager weekly column you sounded exactly like every other adult. For once I'd like to hear someone with a different opinion. Every adult I talk to about drugs wants to lecture me. I don't see how they can give out all this information when they themselves haven't tried it. Not every kid who takes drugs does it to escape reality. Some kids take drugs because of the lectures. I believe kids will take drugs no matter what anyone else says, just because they want to."

Signed (J.S., Cincinnati, Ohio)

My reply was as follows:

"Dear J.S.:
You said you're not interested in the opinion of anyone who hasn't taken dope. Okay, don't take my opinion. But how about advice from a man who was living and breathing and very much alive just one month ago, but who is dead today. He died right here in this prison. He hadn't touched heroin or any drugs for almost ten years. He spent the last ten years of his life fighting to preserve what was left of his body after he stopped taking drugs. He was still a young man in the prime of his life, but heroin and other drugs had effectively destroyed his internal organs and he slowly began to die. When he had finally

realized that he was killing himself with drugs, he tried vainly and desperately to reverse the effects, but the damage had already been done. If I sound like every other adult who preaches to you about drugs it may be because I am in a position to sit here and talk every day with men who have already destroyed their lives, their families, their bodies, with all kinds of drugs from marijuana on up. Sure, you will read and hear a lot of garbage and misinformation about how harmless drugs really are. An opinion such as that is cheap if you don't have to pay the price for being wrong. The man who died here spent his last remaining years visiting schools and outside prison groups, preaching about the deadly effect of drug abuse. He really didn't expect that his own life would end this suddenly.

He believed that the drug addict was trying to escape the "here-and-now" which we call reality. He also believed that most addicts really want to destroy themselves, or their families, or society. Unless you are a confirmed drug addict yourself and can refute this man's lifetime experience and opinions, then I must believe his opinion in the absence of a better one. I can only act as an instrument to pass his views on to you and to your friends. You can accept or reject them as you see fit. But God have mercy on you if you are wrong and he is right. Your body, your life, your future, may be totally ruined.

If there is anything funny or harmless about taking drugs I can't see it. If you think glue-sniffing is cute, what will you tell the child whose liver is now damaged beyond repair from sniffing glue? Would you want your own child someday to destroy himself in this way?

We have thousands of men in our prisons who would willingly give their own lives to help just one teenager to stay off drugs. And what are you willing to give? The least you can do is listen when a dead drug addict talks to you from the grave. He really wants you to live and be happy."

Certainly every person must try to live his life to the best of his ability. True some of us have been more fortunate in our early years than others. But our lives are very much what we make of them. If we decide to turn to crime for quick thrills or easy money, we must also be prepared to pay for this way of life with many boring, wasted years in a dirty, crowded prison cell with other social failures, perhaps listening twenty-four hours a day to the birds outside the cell-block window—birds, incidentally, which we cannot always see. Perhaps the most exciting thing to do under these circumstances would be to count cockroaches as they crawl past the tiny cell, or make a pet of a mouse.

Just before I left prison the last time, I met a guy who impressed me as having the longest prison record of any convict I had ever met. He was thirty-seven years old and his record filled five single-spaced typewritten pages. Before his seventeenth birthday he had been arrested and convicted three times for major crimes. About the only thing that really bothered him, as he told me, was that the other kids at school had never been at all impressed by him. He had spent his school days as a lonely, isolated teenager.

While the other kids studied, he was planning burglaries for that night or for the weekend. While his schoolmates were at the football game, he was roaming the neighborhood, looking for a house to knock over. While other teenagers made friends with each other, he walked alone, friendless and miserable. He despised the other kids, could not bring himself to admit that he, too, needed friendship. It seems odd that this future criminal could be broadcasting so loudly for help and that nobody cared to receive his desperate signals. Apparently he had done a good job of turning everybody off. When the young bully took advantage of younger or weaker students, the other kids just turned their backs on him. It seems that only the principal of his school took any notice of him.

He decided that he'd show them all some day. And that's why he embarked on a deliberate life of crime. You name it, he had done it. Robbery, safecracking, assault, drunken driving and finally, murder with a motor vehicle. The little girl he ran down certainly deserved a better fate than to be killed by the car of a drunken failure.

There are a lot of such potential failures in the schools throughout this country. They need not end up in prison but that's where they are heading if nobody is interested in helping them. Its not just the teacher's responsibility to reach such potentially anti-social young people. You can begin a program of effective crime prevention with your fellow classmates right now. All you need do is take a good look around and seek out those students who appear lost and alone. They are the ones who need friendship to feel that they belong somewhere. Some of these lonely students may scorn your friendship at first, but that's all the more reason to offer it to them. It is easy to reason that they don't deserve your friendship but most kids who get into trouble aren't really bad. They are usually just testing their freedom, trying to see how far they can go before the authorities crack down on them. These students more than any others need to know what it is like to be successful in friendship. And you would have the satisfaction of knowing that you had perhaps helped to prevent a future wasted life of crime. I do not believe that any human being is too far gone for friendship to be wasted on him. Miracles do occur every single day. One of the greatest miracles I have seen is the way in which young people get involved in helping one another. And the remarkable thing is that this pattern of interest and warmth extends and influences others.

I should know. I have been the direct beneficiary of much of that kind of love from the teenage sons and daughters of many of the beautiful people who befriended me when I got out of prison. I am convinced that young people can help cut down crime by helping the lonely kids in their school, neighborhood and home to "belong."

One day while I was working in the prison office, I happened to see a letter that a prison social worker had received from a disturbed father. This man wrote: "Please do something to help my kid. I don't want him to end up in prison." The letter was especially tragic to me because it had been written by a man then serving a sentence in the Ohio Penitentiary. This man had written in desperation to the social worker to get help in preventing his son from following in his footsteps and turning to a life of crime. A lot of convicts I have known feel the same way about kids, all kids, their own and other people's kids. They want to reach out through the bars of their prison cells and with the knowledge that comes of experience, try to convince youth that the cost of crime is too high to pay.

Almost all of us, at some time in our lives, must examine what we stand for. We must take a positive stand for or against certain styles of life. Too many people go through life without examining their ideals or beliefs, without testing them against the realities of existence. In my case, because I made the wrong choices, I ended up in prison. It took me many, many years to realize I had made the wrong choices and to analyze why it was that I had done so. You are still making your choices. I hope you can profit from my experience. It is really up to you.